Coercion and Control in Communist Society

Coercion and Control in Communist Society
The Visible Hand of Bureaucracy

Maria Hirszowicz
Reader in Sociology
University of Reading

Wheatsheaf
Books

DISTRIBUTED BY HARVESTER PRESS

First published in Great Britain in 1986 by
WHEATSHEAF BOOKS LTD
A MEMBER OF THE HARVESTER PRESS PUBLISHING GROUP
Publisher: John Spiers
Director of Publications: Edward Elgar
16 Ship Street, Brighton, Sussex

© Maria Hirszowicz, 1986

British Library Cataloguing in Publication Data
Hirszowicz, Maria
    Coercion and control in Communist society: the visible
    hand of bureaucracy.
    1. Bureaucracy – Communist countries
    I. Title
    350'.001   JC474

    ISBN 0-7450-0071-1

Typeset in 11 on 12pt Times by
Paul Hicks Ltd, Burrington Way, Plymouth, Devon
Printed in Great Britain by Oxford University Press

THE HARVESTER PRESS PUBLISHING GROUP
The Harvester Press Publishing Group comprises Harvester Press
Limited (chiefly publishing literature, fiction, philosophy,
psychology, and science and trade books), Harvester Press
Microform Publications Limited (publishing in microform
unpublished archives, scarce printed sources, and indexes to these
collections) and Wheatsheaf Books Limited (a wholly independent
company chiefly publishing in economics, international politics,
sociology and related social sciences), whose books are distributed
by The Harvester Press Limited and its agencies throughout the
world.

Contents

List of Tables

Preface

The subject of political coercion has concerned me for years. The pattern of my experience was such that it has been impossible not to observe the impact of the coercive bureaucratic rule over economic and social life.

This volume is a follow up to my *Bureaucratic Leviathan;* the generalisations about the nature of Communist societies called for the elaboration of the most important problem of the relationship between political power and economic processes. To elaborate on that topic with regard to the recent Polish crisis I had to link sociology with a number of different disciplines which are usually kept separate. Consequently, I am greatly indebted to many people who were able to give me help and advice about the economic, historical and political aspects of my study.

First and foremost I owe an enormous debt to Włodzimierz Brus, Stanisław Gomułka and Łukasz Hirszowicz who have advised me through the varying phases of analysis and writing. Parts of my book owe a great deal to the advice of Stanisław Gomułka whose assistance in revising the chapter dealing with economic problems in Poland has been immense. Włodzimierz Brus and Łukasz Hirszowicz, who have read my book in draft, helped me to clarify many issues and made many invaluable suggestions which have been implemented in the final version of the study. No words could express my sense of gratitude for their untiring interest and support. I hardly need add that no one but the author is responsible for the views or interpretations presented in this study

I would also like to thank my publisher's reader for perceptive and useful comments upon my manuscript which have helped me to improve it and I have benefited much from the criticism and advice of Mrs Maria Strelcyn and Mrs Helen Chevis who have helped me at various stages of preparing the text for publication.

1 The visible hand of bureaucracy

Most observers of Communist societies believe that the economic development of these countries is seriously impaired by the dictatorial forms of their governments and argue that unhampered economic development will lead to the liberalisation and democratisation of Communist regimes. The multitude of factors which affect social change poses, however, special problems in the study of political processes and forecasting about their possible outcome. Depending on whether one focuses on the technological, economic, social or institutional aspects, differences of opinion will emerge as to the likelihood of Communist societies evolving towards pluralistic democracy.

The main theories which have dealt with those problems show clearly how distinct and even contradictory are the findings about the nature of Communist states and the predictions derived from them. In spite of remarkable progress in the study of Communist systems the basic question about the nature and direction of political change in the Communist world is far from being answered.

There are three main suppositions about the future of Communism. One is the petrification theory which denies the possibility of any substantial changes from within. The other is the convergence theory predicting a gradual 'softening' and pluralisation of the Communist societies. And, finally, the 'class-war' theory looks for the new 'grave-diggers' of Communist dictatorships and finds them in the restless and militant working classes.

The 'petrification theory' is associated with the concept of totalitarianism which had been elaborated with regard to the Stalinist regime and emphasised the similarity of this regime with the Nazi and Fascist models of the all-pervasive party-state. A concise characterisation of totalitarianism elaborated by Coser helps to understand why a totalitarian structure cannot be modified by social forces operating within the system.

1

The essence of totalitarian regimes is that their claims are total; i.e., that they aim at the control of all institutional spheres. . . . Political power has been appropriated by a political élite that suppresses all rival claimants. The political order has unquestioned primacy over all others; no independent organisation, even of an utterly non-political character is allowed to exist. . . . Every social unit must be *gleicheschaltet*; i.e., co-ordinated with the governing apparatus. Insofar as different institutional orders still continue to exist, activities within them are heteronomous; they do not follow laws of motion of their own but are impelled by forces emanating from the political order. Economic agents act in accord with the demands of State and Party, religious institutions become adjuncts to political institutions, and even the family is pressed into the service of political goals. . . . Totalitarian societies destroy traditional social groups, communities, or self-conscious classes and then replace them by new units that are subject to co-ordination and control by state and party. Deprived of the support of non-governmental structures, the individual faces alone the immense tutelary power of the party and state. . . .

Social forces, insofar as they are not driven underground, are no longer antagonistic, the various interests are no longer diversified; indeed, their pressures are mutually reinforcing. The distinction between public and private spheres, central to the liberal model, disappears in totalitarian society. Just as the totalitarian state cannot tolerate autonomous organisations, so it cannot tolerate individual withdrawal into a private— and hence uncontrolled—sphere. (Coser, 1962, p.191)

It seemed obvious at first that systems referred to as totalitarian could not be reformed from within. The historical evidence is evoked to corroborate that view: it is pointed out that both the Nazi and Mussolini's rule collapsed in the course of their military defeat. Yet the Stalinist version of totalitarianism defied that conclusion; after Stalin's death considerable transformations took place both in the USSR and East European countries. The model of totalitarianism was thus denounced as inadequate for the analysis of social change and subsequently the theory of total petrification of Communist societies was dismissed.

The 'convergence theory' which became popular among students of Soviet society adopted a 'developmental model' to account for the evolution of Communist systems. Convergence implied that in the course of advanced industrialisation Western and Communist societies would become more and more alike.

Apart from references to the political culture of Asiatic

empires and East European traditions alien to democratic forms of government, many authors point to the structural and situational factors which favoured the establishment of authoritarian institutions.

Some of the most frequently mentioned internal factors behind the development of Communist dictatorship are:

1) The requirements of primitive accumulation, which imply draconian political measures.

2) The weakness of the working class at the early stages of Communist revolution; the workers are few and too weak as a group to prevent the state and party bureaucracy from substituting their own interests for those of the workers.

3) The conflicting objectives of different groups in society; at the early stage of industrialisation the rule of bureaucracy is necessary to prevent conflicts between the workers and the peasantry and restrain different sectional interests.

The belief in the connection between economic and political progress which will eliminate dictatorial regimes goes back to the argument that there is a functional necessity for advanced industrial societies to develop pluralistic forms of government based on consensus and the rule of law. The conclusion drawn from such arguments is that Communist countries would be capable of balanced development and could guarantee a high living standard provided they carried out democratic reforms of the political systems. It is maintained that if they have not done this so far, the reasons are to be sought in the historical circumstances under which Communism developed.

The convergence theory has been corroborated by a considerable relaxation of the rule of terror in post-Stalinist societies and the evolution of Communist regimes towards forms which could be described as authoritarian power structures.

Following Coser's analysis we would define authoritarian regimes as those which

will attempt to mobilize the citizen in pursuit of their political goals, yet they will not obliterate the distinction between the public and the private sphere—they will leave the latter relatively untouched. The political élite monopolises political power but it shares social powers with the agents of other institutional orders. . . .(Coser, 1962, p.193)

Whereas totalitarian societies suppress all forms of autonomous organisation and all independent sources of information, the authoritarian regimes suppress organised opposition and public criticism. Whereas liberal society fosters the autonomy of the various institutional orders, the authoritarian society limits and confines activities within these orders, but does not attempt to control them completely. Whereas totalitarian societies suppress all conflict among component parts of the social structure, the authoritarian society channels and deflects such conflicts without, however, eliminating them altogether.

In such societies the political powerholders may recognise no constitutional limitations of state power, yet in practice they do recognise *some* limitations. They may try to make the Church into a pliant instrument of their rule, yet they will not attempt to deny the religious order a measure of autonomy in regard to other worldly concerns. They may limit the exercise of proprietary rights and channel the allocation of scarce resources, yet they will not attack the legitimation of property as such. In authoritarian societies the military order is typically somewhat independent of the political order; it may even tend to dominate it. Where totalitarian societies have 'politicised armies', authoritarian societies often have a 'militarised polity'. (Coser, 1962, p.192)

Although there is an almost general consensus about the shift from totalitarianism to authoritarianism in the Communist world, there are far-reaching disagreements about the prospects of further changes.

The convergence theory with its over-optimistic emphasis on the positive impact of technological development has been challenged by class-conflict theory (or theories) based on the assumption that in spite of economic advancement Communist societies will be subject to dictatorial rule as long as the exploited and oppressed masses do not rebel in a class war against their bureaucratic masters.

One points thus to the role of bureaucracy as the new ruling class or classes: once well established in the post-revolutionary order it eliminates and prevents the conception of democratic institutions which could put an end to its domination. The 'red bourgeoisie' is regarded here as the main culprit, the workers as its main victims. The class-war theory could thus be referred to as the 'grave-diggers' theory since it mirrors in minute detail the Marxist scheme of the class war of the proletariat (designated by Marx as the grave-diggers of capitalism) against their capitalist exploiters and oppressors.

The series of crises in Eastern Europe, which have several times shaken the balance of the Communist world, could be regarded as the most convincing evidence of such an approach. The uprising of German workers in 1953, of Polish and Hungarian workers in 1956, the struggle of workers in Czechoslovakia in the years 1968–9 and the explosive confrontations in Poland in 1970, 1976 and 1980–1 epitomise the importance of the 'class-conflict' theory for the understanding of the Communist world.

Yet with respect to the persistence of Communist author-itarianism and the prospect of democratic evolution in the Communist world the class-conflict theory in its present form does not offer much understanding and guidance. It indicates under what conditions the regimes might break down but does not explain why and how they have been able so far to manage internal conflict and does not help to look for programmes of social change short of the revolutionary 'all-or-nothing' strategies.

The underlying assumption in the writings expounding the theories of social change which we have so far discussed is that the coercive components of the Communist states were in the early post-revolutionary years not only unavoidable but to some extent justified by the prevailing circumstances. Externally the power of the Communist state appeared to be the only force able to defend and maintain the proletarian revolution against its enemies; internally it incorporated the drive towards economic and social progress.

In such theories a distinction is drawn between the early stages of Communist revolutions, when the coercive power of the state might have played the role of an instrument of social change, and the advanced, post-Stalinist systems in which dictatorial rule is seen as outdated and disfunctional.

The idea that advanced economy calls, as it were, for the implementation of democratic rule is certainly convincing and appealing by its inherent optimism and belief in the progressive character of social change. It is no wonder that many scholars and politicians, both in the East and West, unreservedly support ideologies based on the belief in the invincibility of democratic principles in the age of advanced industrialism. A closer analysis of the premises on which this outlook is based reveals, however, many weak points which have to be taken into account.

The main argument brought forward quite recently by Clark Kerr, the most prominent spokesman of the optimistic version of the convergence theory, is that of the impact of the possible limitations of economic growth both in the West and East on processes of political change. As he points out, the rate of economic growth remains an overwhelming question for the future. He presents the following scenarios of social development depending on the possible rates of growth.

*Table 1·1 Future scenarios relating rates of growth to direction of movement of social systems**

Toward West package	*Rates of growth and likely direction of social development*	*Toward East package*
←	If generally high (Scenario 1)*	
	If generally low (Scenario 2)	→
	If variable among notions (Scenarios 4, 5 and 6)	
←	where high	
	where low	→
	If negative (Scenario 3)	
	Toward authoritarian and totalitarian systems of the right and left	

See detailed discussion of these scenarios in Kerr (1983), p.120 (reprinted by permission of the publisher).

Another important aspect of the present political regimes in the Communist world has been highlighted by the theory which explains the persistence of dictatorial forms of government by the impact of the division of the world between the superpowers. This explanation, which could be regarded as a modern version of the traditional 'capitalist encirclement theory', points to:

1) The pressure of the technologically superior, hostile environment which strengthens and supports the siege mentality in Communist societies (Bahro, 1981, p.131). The attempts to reform socialism from within are regarded by the Communist parties as activities undermining the existing balance of power in the world which should therefore be 'squeezed out of the system'.

2) The role of the USSR in establishing and maintaining the political systems in Eastern Europe. The USSR has not only initiated their structural assimilation within the Soviet system but has jealously guarded her sphere of influence in Eastern Europe by preventing attempts at independent development.

The differences of economic standards, cultural traditions, and social institutions within the Soviet bloc are much more disruptive and divisive than they would have been in conditions of full autonomy and negotiated agreements. Moreover, there exists something in the modern world which can be called 'the compulsion of comparisons':

We may never reach Sir William Beveridge's utopia where each man could pick and choose around the world the society he would like to live in; but already people are making comparisons, and these comparisons are having their impact. Generally, the impact will be to greater uniformity in the nature of the societal product which people widely judge to be the best. People may not be willing to settle for much less in their own system than the standards and performance of competing systems. (Kerr *et al.*, 1973, p.269).

The built-in conflicts which imply the use of coercion in the Communist world are not confined, however, to the political sphere. The stability of Communist rule depends to a large extent on the extent of control exercised by the Communist party–state over the economy where most serious conflicts arise.

Insofar as the command economy dominates social life *it creates its own contradictions and conflicts which determine the necessity of coercive, dictatorial governments*. This necessity will persist irrespective of the stage of economic development; it is dictated not by technological imperatives, but by the petrification of economic structures within which technology is being utilised and developed.

Some writers would argue that the character of the Communist state is indeed determined by the way Communist economies are run. The most eminent among those who promote such a thesis are F. Hayek and G. Grossman. They both contend that the elimination of the market economy inevitably reinforces and supports the autocratic and all-embracing power of the state. In his book *The Road to Serfdom* Hayek concentrates on the systemic features of an economic organisation based on full nationalisation of the means of production and overall centralised planning.

Planning leads to dictatorship because dictatorship is the most effective instrument of coercion and the enforcement of ideals, and as such is essential if central planning on a large scale is to be possible.' (Hayek, 1976, p.53)

The clash between planning and democracy arises simply from the fact that the latter is an obstacle to the suppression of freedom which the direction of economic activity requires. (ibid., p.52)

The effect of the people agreeing that there must be central planning, without agreeing on the ends, will be rather as if a group of people were to commit themselves to take a journey together without agreeing where they want to go: with the result that they may all have to make a journey which most of them do not want at all. (ibid., p.46)

The whole argument brought forward by Hayek revolves around the consequences of a centralised economy. He is convinced that there is no political freedom without economic freedom. He regards both the USSR and Nazi Germany as examples of 'the non-economic societies of unfreedom'. Central organisation and direction of all social activities, including the economy, meant for him the inevitable rise of totalitarianism. Challenging the socialist doctrine of the necessity of centralised planning in technologically advanced economies, he pointed out that planned society would be an undemocratic society based on arbitrary power of the political authorities.

In a more recent study, *Gold and sword. Money in the Soviet command economy*, Grossman argues that the party and other organs of centralised control and supervision were essential elements of the economic system in which money ceased to regulate the economic activities of people. As far as the local party organs were concerned,

> They thrive on continual local crises. They goad on the sluggish, seek to safeguard the official values and priorities and co-ordinate and expedite things. In other words, they do precisely what active money and its corollaries—equilibrium prices, profit making, market relations, an orderly conduct of affairs—would do for the economy. Passive money equals active party. (Grossman, 1966, p.235)

The importance of the arguments presented by Hayek and Grossman lies in their emphasis on the close links between economy and politics. Their demarcation line runs between market economy and command economy, the former being associated with democratic forms of government. Once market forces are eliminated and the means of production are subject to centralised management, the state cannot operate according to democratic principles. This view clashes with the opinions that totalitarianism and authoritarianism in the Communist world are passing phenomena.

The essence of Hayek's and Grossman's generalisations about the political systems in Communist societies can be presented as a simple scheme:

Centralised economy→ Totalitarianism (or party–state
authoritarianism)

This scheme can be further developed by adding new variables which take into account other forces interfering in the relationship between politics and economy. Our scheme will include social conflicts as the correlation of economies run in a centralised way.

Command economy → Coercive state
└→ Social conflicts─┘

The general propositions regarding the possibility of conflicts and their intensity can tentatively be presented as follows:

1) The more numerous the situations in which one side interferes in the affairs of the other, the more likely are conflicts of interest between them.
2) The greater the disparity of objectives pursued by the groups concerned, the more likely are conflicts between them.
3) The more likely the superimposition of different types of conflicts between the same groups, the more intensive the conflict becomes.
4) The less developed the channels of communication between the parties involved in a conflict, the less likely the resolution of that conflict through negotiation and compromise.

It follows from the first proposition that Communist economies have a high potential for generating conflicts between the rulers and the ruled. Communist bureaucracies carry out incomparably more functions in regulating and co-ordinating economic and social activities than past forms of government. The further the government expands its functions in regulating the economy, the more it interferes with people's interests and the more likely people will try to influence those decisions which are important to them.

All depends, however, on the degree of convergence or divergence between the objectives pursued by the party–state bureaucracy and the interests of the masses. The second proposition cannot therefore be applied to Communist or other societies as self-evident. There are many authoritarian structures in which conflicts can be avoided because the interests of the rulers and ruled largely coincide. Many advocates of Communism argue that this would be the case at the more advanced stage of development of the Communist economy when growing affluence will eliminate the causes of social discontent.

There is ample evidence, however, that Communist societies generate deep social conflicts irrespective of the stage of technological development. The nature of these conflicts is to be sought in the new divisions which characterise Communist economies and the contradictions arising out of them.

It seems paradoxical to refer to divisions in systems which were supposed to eliminate the fragmentation of the capitalist economy and the class war between the owners of the means of production and the workers. Yet, contrary to optimistic expectations, old divisions have been replaced by new ones.

The party–state economy is characterised by a far-reaching unification of all economic activities which were fragmented under the conditions of the free market. At the same time this very unification generates the separation of many economic processes which were closely interlinked within the market economy, and creates new forms of fragmentation and incoherence of economic activities which, if left unrestrained, can lead to economic crisis.

THE SEPARATION OF PRODUCTION FROM CONSUMPTION

In a market economy production is, albeit in a very imperfect way, closely linked to the pattern and volume of consumption. Producers try to manufacture what they think will sell and any wider discrepancy between supply and demand activates mechanisms of adjustment: rising prices and increased production if the demand outpaces supply, falling prices and reduced production if the supply is excessive.

In a command economy the central planner can set up economic objectives without paying attention to the needs of the consumers and frequently ignoring even the demands of the producers' market. The mismatch of what is produced with what is needed occurs both on the macro- and micro-level, generating on the one hand wastage of raw materials and human resources, on the other hand acute shortages. The resulting imbalances are usually dealt with at the expense of the consumer market: whenever the production of the means of production and the operations of key industries are threatened by insufficient supplies the central planner will carry out the necessary adjustments by drastic cuts in the resources serving the consumer market.

The separation of central economic decisions from the responsibility for their implementation

The disfunction caused by the arbitrariness of central planners is reinforced by the fact that those who make large-scale decisions are not responsible for their implementation, which is left to individual firms and enterprises. If the relevant industries fail to attain the planned objectives they are the only ones to be blamed even if the attainment of these objectives was from the start beyond their reach. This results in lack of concern of the planning authorities for the cost of maximisation of the plans—a phenomenon labelled, in the Communist vocabulary, economic voluntarism.

The separation of the costs from market prices constitutes another factor potentially contributing to the imbalances:

a) Since the cost of investments is irrelevant for the prices of the final products investments can be planned without much regard to their economic effectiveness.

b) The heavily subsidised prices of some raw materials and basic consumer goods contribute on the one hand to the chronic wastage of labour and material resources and, on the other hand, tend to create excessive demand and chronic shortages of goods which can be bought for a song. The balance of the spending power of the population is achieved in such circumstances by overpricing of some other products and a constant pressure on the level of incomes.

These factors, combined with an authoritarian power structure which deprives the population of direct involvement in the decision-making process, generate a phenomenon of self-consuming growth characterised by industry working for industry while the consumers' market is usually neglected. As some people in Poland used to say, 'industry is eating its own tail'; such a situation will occur when increases in production potential do not result in any improvement in living standards because the increased volume of production is largely being recycled into the producers' market. It may even happen that economic growth will be associated with the decrease of consumption because of the growing depletion of resources redirected from the consumers' to the producers' market.

It has generally been assumed that the priority given to heavy industry is the main reason for the phenomenon of self-consuming growth. It seems, however, that this is not necessarily the case. Recent evidence suggests that even in conditions where growth is apparently oriented towards the needs of the consumer there are systemic factors which distort the balance on behalf of the producers. In such a system imbalance is endemic and, if left unchecked, tends to create a serious obstacle to economic development. Depletion of the consumer market undermines the value of wages, and inadequate performance of light industries affects, in the long run, supplies for the key sectors of the economy. All this would make the system very unstable and subject to permanent disruptions were it not for safeguards built into it, preventing the economy from progressing from one crisis to another.

The coercive power of the state prevents people from resisting economic policies which affect the quality of their life. Bans on strikes, the absence of free trade unions and severe penalties for the dissemination of unauthorised publications are effective barriers to manifestations of public discontent about economic policies. The role of coercion increases when the restoration of balance on the consumer market requires substantial cuts in the real incomes of the population, mostly achieved by price rises, currency reforms, compulsory loans, etc.

Control of the instruments of coercion allows the goverment to enforce a compliance which would not have been achieved otherwise. People have to put up with shortages, accept price increases and tolerate a reduction of their living standards. They have no option but to refrain from wage claims and even endure cuts in their earnings when the authorities deem it necessary for the maintenance of economic balance. When their patience and endurance are eroded they are faced with the full force of the police and the army.

Coercion is thus the major component in regulating economic behaviour to conform with the strategies and policies of central government and a necessary ingredient of a relatively balanced development. If we apply the renowned concept of the invisible hand to characterise the forces controlling free-market economy, *it is the visible hand of bureaucracy which directs and regulates economic activity not only by administrative but also by coercive means.*

While the market economy enforces compliance and co-operation of producers by competition, raising or falling profits, unemployment and crises, the command economy has to resort to the power of the coercive state. Hence, a regime using, when necessary, naked power is an indispensable correlative of bureaucratically managed economies. The coercive power of the party–state is essential not only in the role of midwife, helping the birth of a new economic and social order (Marx), but in the everyday functioning of the Communist system no matter how well established and economically advanced it is.

It should be noted that the so-called Communist hardliners make no bones about the fact that far from being a mere relic of the past, redundant at a more advanced stage of economic development, coercion is an indispensable feature of Communist societies.

Stalin rejected as utter rubbish the theory of the withering away of the state and did his best to utilise coercive power to eradicate any signs of resistance or deviance. His heirs have been more moderate and selective in applying heavy-handed measures and have been prepared to refine the mechanisms of control over society to make them less obtrusive and severe, but when it comes to essential issues they do not hesitate to resort to naked power. In most cases the mere threat of such measures is sufficient to keep society in check. When this does not suffice the sword becomes the final instrument of normalisation, a euphemism for the restoration of order after a mass upheaval.

However, the Stalinist and neo-Stalinist medicine for the shortcomings of the system contains seeds of further conflicts. In so far as economic decisions are concentrated at the top, that is, in the hands of the central political leadership, the intensified superimposition of politics onto economic conflict is inevitable. Because dictatorial rule deprives society of effective channels to articulate grievances and negotiate their resolution this means that any conflict is potentially lethal for the system: the masses have no other means of expressing their discontent but by occupying factories, coming out on to the streets and resorting to violence, a situation which makes the state determined to increase coercive measures so as to nip all resistance in the bud.

The conflicts in the economic sphere are intensified by and overlap with political grievances because of growing social inequality and administrative privilege which increase with the economic development of Communist societies.

Wesołowski argues that these grievances also are directed against the authorities.

In socialist society the unequal distribution of goods in high demand is made through the mechanism of governmental decisions . . . the government assumes the role of direct regulator. This explains a special psychological situation. People with insufficient incomes tend to blame the government (as the regulator of incomes) rather than the more favoured groups. (Wesołowski, 1972, p.138)

The situation becomes even more complicated when Communist governments try to improve the supply of many commodities by tolerating or even encouraging the development of the private sector. A parallel private market invariably generates staggering disparities in incomes. Moreover, administrative corruption grows in proportion to the development of the private sector: the dependence of private producers on supplies regulated by state functionaries inevitably breeds corruption.

As long as the economic situation is relatively stable, people tolerate both economic inequality and bureaucratic corruption as part of the system. But when the economic situation deteriorates, both issues become explosive and intensify the rebellion directed against the complacent and inefficient government.

In view of the many contradictions built into the Communist economy, one of the main preoccupations of the party–state apparatus is preventing political conflicts from coming out into the open. On the ideological level the myth of conflict-free development is, of course, sustained and cultivated. Solidarity is a battle cry of the party mobilising support against the enemies of socialism within and without. At the same time no other issue is more important than the wiping out of deviation and dissent by all possible means, including the use of naked power when necessary.

The whole doctrine of Communism is based on regarding violence and coercion as the vehicle of human history. For Marx the state was synonymous with bureaucratic military machinery in the hands of the ruling class. Its major function was the defence of a social organisation which protected the interests of the privileged minority. Referring to centralised state power, Marx pointed to 'its ubiquitous organs of standing army, police, bureaucracy, clergy and judicature' (Jordan, 1971, p.274).

Lenin followed the same line. He insisted that the state was the organisation of naked power in the hands of the ruling minority, and consisted primarily of 'gangs of armed men' i.e., the police and military. While Durkheim based his notion of the state on the idea of functionaries carrying out general administrative tasks and Weber emphasised the legitimisation of the monopoly of power as the attribute of the state, revolutionary Marxists insist that 'might makes right'; monopolistic control over the means of physical coercion within a given territory constitutes the essence of the state. They argue that the legitimisation of the existing power structure by the constitutional charter is nothing else but the outward expansion of the monopoly of power of the ruling classes which allows them to create and enforce laws which protect them. Many political scientists nowadays would agree with that view. As Wrong argues: 'political institutions are, in fact, most clearly differentiated from other institutions by virtue of their monopolistic control of the means of coercion.' (Wrong, 1979, p.43)

It should be noted that the characteristic trait of the Communist party–state is its capacity to combine control of the military and police force with other resources of power over society. A whole range of controls includes:

a) coercive power of the military and police;
b) economic power with control over means of production and distribution of benefits;
c) 'political power with control over legitimate and ultimate decision-making within a specified territory';
d) 'ideological power involving control over belief and value systems, religion, education, specialised knowledge and propaganda';
e) 'diversionary power with control over hedonistic interests, recreation and enjoyment'.

(see Schermerhorn, 1964, p.17)

All these instruments of power can indeed be utilised to secure compliance and eliminate dissent. There are situations, however, when they are ineffective. It is then that a political crisis develops.

Let us look at the sequence of political crises in Eastern Europe after Stalin

Table 1·2 Political crises in Eastern Europe, 1953–80

Country	Year of political crisis
Germany	1953
Poland	1956
Hungary	1956
Czechoslovakia	1968
Poland	1970
Poland	1976
Poland	1980

The list shows that in spite of the power of political regimes in Eastern Europe, they are unable to prevent outbursts of mass discontent. It is also obvious that the solution of political crises is sought rather by resorting to naked power than to concessions and negotiated agreement. 'As an alternative to bargaining, coercion can be construed as an attempt by its user to gain compliance or concessions from an opponent without giving anything in return.' (Bachrach and Lawler, 1981, p.171)

Apart from Poland in 1956, 1970 and 1976, all political crises in Eastern Europe have been solved by military means and Poland herself finally fell victim to coercive measures in 1981.

There is, of course, the Russian factor which explains that pattern. The Russian intervention in Hungary and Czechoslovakia and the threat of such an intervention in Poland in 1981, which left the Polish leadership with no option but to carry out the military coup on their own, do not leave any doubts about the ability of the Soviet power to block all political reforms within the Russian empire. One could expect, however, that one day the Soviet regime might be faced by a similar crisis without anyone to come to its rescue. Many observers in East Europe expect that such a situation will occur sooner or later leaving the Soviet regime with no choice but to negotiate with their own masses or to succumb to their numerical superiority.

Such predictions, whether applied to the Soviet regime or to East European societies, do not take into account those integrative and regulative forces and mechanisms in Communist societies which determine and support their resistance to change. The three main factors which we shall discuss in more detail are:

    (a) the 'no-surrender' policies of the ruling institutions, legitimised by the dual functions they carry out with regard to society;

    (b) the systemic instability of the bureaucratic power structure;

    (c) the self-defeating consequences of negotiated settlements of political crises.

(a) The vested interests supporting the Communist establishment are conventionally presented in terms of class theory. The ruling class, defined by some as the 'nomenclature' class is supposed to defend the establishment because of the power, material privilege and prestige bestowed upon those who belong to it. What is often ignored is the fact that support for the existing regime is at least partly generated because of the vital managerial and administrative functions the party–state bureaucracy carries out. Even the political opponents of the regime have to co-operate with it as employees serving society in their professional and vocational capacities.

The difference between ruling institutions and ruling classes may seem of purely academic interest, but in fact is extremely important. A ruling institution—be it the church in theocracies, the army in military societies, or the party in one-party states—identifies not with an economic but with a political order which gives it the dominant position in society. In contrast to economic classes which see in politics the reinforcement of their economic privileges, the ruling institutions treat economic systems as instrumental in the maintenance of their position of power.

If we define control as

a process that includes planning—the setting of goals, objectives and standards; establishing procedures designed to meet the goal and objectives; data gathering and feedback systems to indicate when standards and objectives are being met; and systems of action to reduce any deviations from the chartered course (Mitchell, 1982, p.350)

it is obvious that in a democratic system not only does the state control society but society controls the state. It is also obvious that although such a relationship is symmetrical, each has a vested interest in retaining its autonomy and increasing its influence over the other.

In an asymmetrical relationship in which the party–state institution dominates society, the urge to maintain power over society meets no counterforces to restrain it. At the same time the importance of the functions central authorities fulfil in regulating and co-ordinating social life legitimises their power. In contrast to foreign occupation when overt force is used to extort as much as possible from the enslaved society, Communist regimes carry out innumerable functions on behalf of their subjects and present themselves as 'ruling servants' in a society built allegedly on solidarity principles.

When the ruling institutions resort to violence in response to mass demands they justify their actions by the need to fight against anarchy and defend their country against external enemies, an argument which appeals not only to the privileged stratum but to wider society as well, so long as no viable alternatives to Communist rule exist.

(b) Contrary to the view that the party–state bureaucracy is totally committed to the Communist establishment, its compliance and identification with the ruling institutions cannot be taken for granted.

The functionaries of the state apparatus differ greatly in their attitude to the establishment. Some of them will fully identify with the interests of the institutions they work for, others will not. Some will behave like devoted servants, others like modern mercenaries motivated primarily by greed and, at the best, professional pride. Dual allegiance to the party and state apparatus does not change that picture; membership of the party is the price one has to pay for access to many administrative jobs, a price which implies some outward manifestations of loyalty to the party élites and their policy, but no more than that. Whether such loyalty is sustained in a situation of a political crisis is another matter. In normal circumstances the party–state apparatus acts as a centrally operated machine; the functionaries follow orders and carry out their tasks because they are paid and rewarded for so doing and punished when they fail to satisfy their superiors. Their compliance is reinforced by administrative privileges and other benefits associated with their positions in the party–state apparatus and by a complex system of mechanisms of control monitoring all bureaucratic activities.

As long as organisational pressures within the state apparatus operate effectively the ruling élites retain full control over the members of the party–state institutions, but the situation changes drastically—as most political crises reveal—when Communist rule is challenged by mass movements. Such a situation invariably affects the balance of forces within the party–state apparatus itself and therefore threatens the very foundations of existing power structure. Centralised control becomes difficult, sanctions ineffective, routines pointless and counterproductive. A political crisis gives not only more power to the masses owing to their superiority in numbers, but affects the cohesiveness and unity of the party–state apparatus in which many members of the bureaucracy and many party functionaries change their allegiance and support the rebellious masses. It is in such a situation that the myth of the party–state bureaucracy as the ruling class is clearly disproved.

It follows that the ruling élites have to control society as a whole if they want to control their own lower and intermediary supporters. Coercion appears in that context as an integrative force not only on the societal but also on the institutional level. Its latent function is the reinforcement of the cohesiveness and reliability of the ruling institutions by reducing the range of the options of those who serve them and maintaining their dependence on the establishment.

The Communist élites will thus have to apply preventive measures as soon as they are faced by a threat of political crisis. Once they allow the crisis to escalate they can expect the erosion of the very foundations on which their power rests. Their own rank and file will split, many of them joining the rebels, and some 'nomenclature' functionaries will opt for serving new masters. If the crisis is not solved by a prompt intervention of military power, even amidst the ranks of the ruling élites there will be some who identify with the causes of the mass movement.

(c) What happens, however, if for one reason or another the Communist élites do not respond to a political crisis by a display of coercive power but decide to look for negotiated or tacit agreements? It will be argued in this study that so far such agreements and concessions—because of the nature of the system—have generated even deeper and more serious economic and political imbalances.

Up to 1981 Poland appeared to be a country in which political crises ended not with intervention but with concessions to the demands of the masses. Yet at the same time Poland has been the only country in the Communist bloc where crises have occurred with striking regularity. Would there be a connection between these two aspects of Polish history? An important observation in this respect was made by R. Portes. He pointed out that inflationary processes in Poland were caused not merely by the economic and political mistakes of the authorities, but by 'their relative lack of authority itself' (Portes, 1978, p.85). He argued:

Throughout the post-war period, Poland has had overall the weakest monetary management among the CPEs. This may be attributable in part to weakness in Party control over society. These are evident in the Party's inability to eliminate the influence of the Church or to impose the collectivisation of agriculture; and culturally and politically, many have continued to look to the West, regarding the Party as the unfortunate but perhaps indispensable buffer against direct Soviet rule. . . . Industrial workers in Poland are now fully conscious of their political strength and they will resist any belt-tightening—any effort to make them repeat the restraint of the late 1960s. The planners' freedom of action is severely constrained (ibid.).

And indeed the weakness of Polish authoritarianism has a long record beginning after. Stalin's death.

1) Poland has been the only country (apart from Yugoslavia) in which Sovietisation was not fully implemented;

2) Poland has been the only country in East Europe where up to a certain point the authorities conceded the demands of the masses;

3) Poland is the largest of the East European countries, which made external threat of intervention more difficult to carry out unless absolutely necessary.

One could conclude that Poland exemplifies a country in which for historical reasons the control of the party–state over society was subject to far-reaching constraints, where the negative power of the masses proved sufficient to block many of the centrally promoted policies and where at the same time external constraints did not allow for any basic reforms of the system, all of which made Poland the most imbalanced part of the Communist bloc.

2 Poland's recurring crises: theory and history

FROM UNMASKING TO UNDERSTANDING

Explanations of the present economic and political situation in Poland oscillate between 'pure theory' and 'pure history'. Some observers of the recent crisis in Poland look at it within the context of other crises which have been taking place in Eastern Europe and in Poland since the Second World War. Others concentrate on the unique and specific features of the development of Poland without paying much attention to its systemic features.

The first approach leads invariably to over-generalisations because the specific traits of Polish history and Polish society are disregarded. The second tends to overlook those traits of Communism which are common to all East European societies, irrespective of the historical differences between them.

The disparity between 'pure theory' and 'pure history' manifests itself in many discussions which take place in Poland, where the desire to explain the sources of the present crisis is understandably an imperative one. The ideological warfare in Poland today makes these discussions even more difficult.

We face in Poland a classic situation described by Zinoview: on the one hand we find there the apologetic approach promoted by official propaganda which tries to hide as far as possible the ugly face of the system; on the other hand the 'unmasking' approach directly reveals the ugly face of the system without much concern for anything else. But, as Zinoview argues:

understanding a society is not the same as unmasking its defects. Unmasking is negative: understanding positive. Unmasking affects the emotions; understanding is exclusively in the realm of reason. . . . Unmasking may be the enemy of understanding no less than apologetics. (Zinoview, 1984, p.14)

The apologetic approach to Polish crises will express itself in attempts to dismiss the view that there are any systemic features which make such crises inevitable or possible. This is being done by putting the blame on successive leaders who, according to official propaganda, were in each case responsible for the outbreak of the crisis. Thus, Gomułka is accused of having caused the eruption of 1970, and Gierek is blamed for the years 1976 and 1980. Gierek and his closest associates are accused of practically everything that happened in Poland in 1970–80, not only by Polish Communists but more and more often by official Soviet propaganda.

The party CC states that it is impossible to postpone an assessment of Comrade Edward Gierek's responsibility any longer. For more than nine years he was First Secretary of the CC. Many correct and socially accepted decisions and political, social and economic ventures in the seventies were made on his initiative and with his participation. This applies in particular to bringing the country out of the December crisis and starting and developing a number of economic and social programmes. At the same time, he bears serious personal responsibility for arbitrariness in economic and social policy, for ignoring economic laws and disregarding critical opinions. (Warsaw Home Service, 3 December 1980.)

A more sophisticated version of the apologetic approach is that of blaming Stalin and the pro-Stalinist faction in the Polish Communist Party for diverting Poland from the course of genuinely Polish socialism. An elaborate theory of the Polish crises along those lines has been presented by a prominent Communist Party ideologist, Andrzej Werblan, who argued that the causes of the present crisis were to be found in the changes which took place in 1947–8, when Gomułka was accused of rightist nationalist deviation, removed from his post of First Party Secretary, the leadership being taken over by a group of Stalinists carrying out Stalin's policy in Poland.

In 1968 Werblan promoted his views on the decisive impact on Polish history of the 1948 crisis in order to discredit the Jews, who by that time were accused by him of having destroyed the positive traditions of Polish Communism (Werblan, 1968). Twelve years later he dropped his argument about the responsibility of the Jews for having supported Stalinism in Poland and concentrated on the adverse effects of the 1948 political overturn on the style of leadership of the Communist Party.

According to Werblan, all successive crises in Poland, besides having certain specific features, are characterised by a discrepancy between new political, social and economic problems and the power structure which imposes limitations on the ways crises can be solved (Werblan, 1981).

Contradictions manifesting themselves in the years 1956, 1970, 1976 and 1980 are regarded by Werblan as the inevitable outcome of the industrialisation of Poland, in the course of which workers and intelligentsia became emancipated and developed new aspirations and demands. The ruling élites were unable to respond to the rising expectations: the will to carry out substantial reforms was lacking and revisionist ideas, substituted for the demands of the masses, harmed the party and destabilised the system.

The views expressed by Werblan and many other party ideologists convey a double message: on the one hand there is the admission that things have gone wrong because the version of Communism adopted in Poland did not correspond to Polish traditions and aspirations, on the other hand there is a hint that it was primarily the evil force personified by Stalin which led Poland from the path of Communism with a human face. The party and its élite are presented as the victims of alien pressure, the responsibility of those who supported Stalinisation is not admitted (apart from those' of Jewish background who fit the description of alien outsiders), nor is any reference made to all those activists who, after Stalin's death, opposed de-Stalinisation in 1955–7 and blocked the attempts at democratic reforms in 1968 and in the early 1970s.

Professor W. Markiewicz, a leading Polish Marxist, summarised these views when he stated without any comment that

More and more numerous are the adherents of the thesis that the sources of deformations which brought about the alienation of the party and in particular of its leading and middle cadres are to be sought not in the last decade but in much earlier times, probably in 1948. It was then, with the declaration of the accusations against the so-called nationalist and rightist deviation, that the centralised and bureaucratic model of party and government was adopted, a model which was contrary to the traditions of Polish political culture, and which has never been subsequently modified. (Markiewicz, 1981)

An attempt to defend the major values of the Communist system while at the same time unmasking some of its unpleasant features has found its expression in those views which point out that Polish crises have grown in the soil of alienation and bureaucratic ossification.

Criticism of the bureaucratic ossification of the political system appeared relatively early in the Polish Communist Party—its roots are to be found in Trotsky's writings. Ochab, at the 7th Plenary Session of the Central Committee in 1956, pointed to the contradiction between the rapid development of the material and spiritual needs of the nation, and the over-centralised, bureaucratic forms of economic management and political organisation. References to alienation were numerous in the years 1956–8, and were revived in the discussion of the 1980–1 crisis.

It should be noted, however, that the presentation of the revisionist line by some journalists in the Communist press was anaemic and reflected the fossilisation of political thought within the party. Alienated bureaucracy was declared the culprit for what had happened, without any serious attempts to reveal the systemic causes of the crises. Verbal accusations directed against bureaucracy for neglecting the needs of the masses and destroying the bond between the party and the working class were vague and much too general to help in identifying the mechanisms which led to the crisis.

One Polish journalist directly stated, for example, that the bureaucratic apparatus of the party and state had developed into an alienated system dominating society and neglecting the interests and demands of the masses. He pointed out that each of the crises was accompanied by signs of spiralling alienation leading to the dissipation of the potential of the socialist system (Krasucki, 1981).

Another writer pointed out that Polish history after 1945 was characterised by an increasing resistance of the working class and society at large to the maladministration of the ruling bureaucracies, and distinguished three different phases in which bureaucracy dominated Polish society:

1) The first stage in which bureaucratic rule was practically unchallenged—a situation explained partly by a shortage of leading cadres, weakness of the institutions of socialist democracy and deviations from socialist ideology.

2) The second stage in which the role of bureaucracy was limited partly by the pressure of the working class and the short-lived workers' councils, and partly by the development and maturing of society as a whole.

3) The third stage under Gierek when bureaucracy took control of the carrying out of reforms under the pressure of the masses. The attempts to effect these reforms failed partly because of the ill-thought-out plan of decentralisation, and partly because of the peculiar mixture of the command and market economy (Krawczewski, 1981).

There were many similar views expressed in the leading organs of the press in 1980-1. They had one thing in common: the avoidance of any accusations directed against party political rule. The crises in Poland could thus be presented as an unacceptable deviation from the right and inevitable march towards socialism under the guidance of the Communist Party, which at each stage was able to recognise its own mistakes and correct them.

In contrast to the above-mentioned views which could be labelled as pseudo-revisionism or mock-revisionism (as compared with the revisionism of the past), members of the political opposition who discussed the crises emphasised that the main conflict in Poland had always been between the party and society, and especially the party and the workers, and pointed out that the main feature of a crisis was that it brought such conflicts into the open.

Jakub Karpiński, who published several books dealing with the successive political crises in Poland, points out (1981) that the main social conflict in Poland is between the party and the workers. The conflict has always existed in its latent form, and a crisis brought it into the open. The common characteristics of the successive political crises are the following:

a) The workers' protests are triggered off every time by the party leaders' decisions. These decisions happened to be directed against the workers' vital interests.

b) Every time, the crisis started as a strike in one factory and gradually spread over a wider area and in some cases over the whole country.

c) Every time, with the exception of 1976, the workers went beyond purely economic demands and pressed for radical social and political reforms.

d) In each case, with the exception of 1980–1, street demonstrations were taking place so that the government had to revert to repressive measures.

e) The use of force was every time combined with an ideological campaign, emphasising the anti-socialist character of the workers' revolt.

f) In each case, confrontation and repressions were followed by considerable concessions to mass demands, economic reforms were carried out and decisions which had triggered the resistance of the workers were altered.

Jakub Karpiński states that in all the crises he described and analysed, the workers' rebellion generated some sort of a cycle which invariably went through the following stages: protest, repression, propaganda smear campaign, reshuffle of the leading cadres, reforms and liberalisation, followed after some time by a gradual withdrawal of the conciliatory changes under the pressure of the party apparatus. A full cycle generated, in other words, the likelihood of a new conflict which sooner or later would reappear on the surface in an open rebellion (Karpiński, 1981).

A theory of the development of the crises has been elaborated by Władysław Bieńkowski, a prominent Polish dissident scholar who traced the roots of the last and earlier crises to the nature of the political system imposed and maintained by the party since 1945 (Bieńkowski, 1980).

Bieńkowski sees the main contradiction as the contradiction between the powerholders—i.e., the party as an institution—and society. What the party presents as passing errors and deviations is in fact a continuous process of pernicious policies carried out by the party from 1945 and interrupted only temporarily by the pressures of the masses in 1956, i.e., during the so-called Polish October, in 1970, when some processes of reconstruction were initiated as a response to the 1970 riots, and in 1980. So far the party has every time managed to stop the attempts at serious economic and political reforms and to restore the authoritarian power structure.

The system in which the party is the ruling institution has replaced the division of power between the legislative, executive and judicial branches of government as in the democratic order. The same individuals who make decisions, control themselves and apply the laws they themselves created to regulate their own activities.

The basic weakness of this system is the petrification of party rule. The party is unable to make any creative innovations and to build up any programme for the future. Since all attempts to change this situation were destroyed by the party itself, the state of the economy was bound to deteriorate in parallel with the growing complexity of economic activities. The command economy is unable to cope with processes of economic growth in an effective way—on the contrary, it aggravates the difficulties and creates a permanent imbalance between different economic sectors which affects the living standards of the population. Important areas of economic activities are neglected, key industries are developed at the expense of others regarded as less relevant to the needs of a socialist economy, self-regulating mechanisms are destroyed and all creative drives and initiatives on the micro- and macro-scales are eliminated.

The vested interests of the party as the ruling institution are thus the cause of the evil. The author, a former member of the Communist élite, thus blames Communism as a system and sees the victory of society over Communist domination as the only effective way of breaking the pattern of crisis development.

It is, of course, impossible in a short outline to cover the whole spectrum of views which have been presented in Poland in the course of the debate on the recurring crises.

To elaborate on our formula 'from unmasking to understanding' we have to mention, albeit very briefly, the
comprehensive theories of the crises elaborated by some
prominent economists and sociologists in Poland.

The economists did not fail to notice that political unrest
in 1955–6, 1970, 1976 and 1980 was associated on each
occasion with serious economic difficulties, and they are
inclined to believe that economic cycles account for the
instability of the political climate in Poland.

Some time before the political crisis of 1980 began, a
group of Polish economists presented an interesting analysis
of the cyclical development of the Polish economy (Gościn-
ski *et al.*, 1981, a,b,c). They saw three stages in each cycle:

1) A stage of accelerated industrialisation based on the
utilisation of existing reserves.

2) A stage in which, after reserves have been exhausted,
industrialisation creates a deep imbalance in the economy by
absorbing more and more raw materials, power supplies,
profits from export and labour. The further this process
advances, the greater the imbalance becomes, and the result
is an inflationary increase in the money supply. Many
investment projects fail to be completed, the discipline of
work deteriorates and increases in wages are not matched by
adequate supplies of market commodities.

3) The third stage begins when the authorities try to
restore the balance by lowering the planned objectives,
cutting investment and imposing restrictions on currency
expenditure, wages and employment. The gap between
demand and supply grows even further and a deterioration
in the overall living standards and employment opportunities creates social tensions and political unrest.

The authors pointed out that these cycles and the resulting
political crises are due to the rigidity of the administrative
mechanisms which distort the implementation of planned
objectives and trigger uncontrolled mechanisms of accelerated industrialisation. Reforms of the system are difficult to
carry out since bureaucratic management enforces its own
priorities, and protects vested interests and cliques.

The study emphasises that the system of economic
organisation in Poland has remained practically intact since

1958. It is based on the following principles: (a) the corporation dominates individual enterprises; (b) no independent enterprises can exist outside corporations; (c) corporations embrace enterprises producing similar final products i.e., they create a monopoly of producers over the market.

The political authorities somehow have a built-in tendency to enforce a maximal rate of growth. In pursuing this tendency one creates a climate of fascination with the maximisation of growth of the national income and of the global product. In this spirit and in these terms the successes of catching up with the most developed countries are measured and expressed. It is a kind of 'overheating' of the economy by creating investment booms which undermine the balance of the system.

The fundamental tendency consists then of enforcement of the maximum rate of growth and this is done without any regard to trends in the world economy, especially in the developed countries. Central authorities tend to overestimate the impact of this growth on development and at the same time they tend to underestimate the impact of physical limitations (raw materials, investment funds, etc.) and of economic and social constraints.

It is pointed out that the high rate of growth very quickly eats up the reserves which existed at the beginning of the rapid acceleration. The whole strategy was based on the assumptions that (a) social and economic processes can be fully controlled; and (b) the authorities have a full knowledge of the processes they direct. Both assumptions are erroneous and activities based on these assumptions have a negative effect on the economy as a whole (*Życie i Nowoczesność*, 26 February, 1981). The authors argue that the mechanisms of the market cannot operate properly and all attempts to utilise them invariably fail. In Poland the rigid structure of the command economy is reinforced by the growing concentration of industry: the number of enterprises diminished from 3,514 in 1966 to 2,849 in 1977 while their production trebled and employment grew by 60 per cent. The number of plants increased at the same time from 15,500 to 18,600.

A different line of economic analysis is presented by those authors who are inclined to believe that the 1980 crisis had a special character and cannot be compared with the previous ones. Z. Mikołajczyk (1981) in an article, 'Rudimentary comments about the crisis', argues for instance that the years 1944-80 were characterised by extensive development which allowed for the increasing satisfaction of social needs, and was therefore tolerated by the majority of working people, as long as some reforms and readjustments were implemented.

The years 1945–9 brought a rapid reconstruction of the post-war economy. The rapid industrialisation which followed ended with necessary readjustment and social reforms which brought a certain increase in living standards and some democratisation of the system.

In the years 1956–70 the economic benefits of the rapid industrial advancement of earlier years came to fruition, but the available resources were gradually exhausted while the aspirations of the population grew and reflected the economic and cultural advancement of urban industrial groups in society.

After 1970 new reserves of extensive development were mobilised, including reserves in agriculture, increases in employment, imports, investments and foreign loans. The attempts at limited reform failed in 1976, and since then the outbreak of the final crisis was a matter of time. In 1980 the disproportions in the economy and the social tensions reached their limits but this time resources allowing for new partial readjustments were completely exhausted.

Why, asks the author, has the extensive development dominated so far over the intensive one? The answer is that the former is based on the availability of resources and as long as these resources were available, as happened in Poland up to 1976, the search for alternative strategies could have been avoided. On the other hand, intensive development implies knowledge of the economic situation, the ability to control this situation, the elaboration of concepts and theories, adequate prices, social support, discipline, etc. That is, it requires considerable political changes which, one could conclude, are incompatible with the interests of the establishment.

A wider economic theory of crises has been put forward in a book by a well-known economist, Józef Pajestka (1981). Pajestka presents socialism as an attempt to embody the ideology of progress. He points out that this ideology is imposed by people who are determined to use power as a lever for social transformation. Socialism is, in other words, not a product of structural evolution but a result of revolution carried out from above. Its advocates are inclined to believe that the new system embodies the idea of progress, and is able, therefore, to satisfy all human needs. Since these hopes do not and cannot materialise, the critics of socialism assume that the reverse is true, that is, that socialism fails altogether and contradicts any chance of progressive development.

Another consequence of the idea of progress implemented by revolution from above, is the conviction that the powerholders who implement the socialist idea are endowed with an almost divine right to carry out their objectives, and to impose their will on society. Their programme consists in the first place of rapid industrialisation. The heavy burden of investments enforced by such a programme is contrary to the expectations and aspirations of the masses and generates resistance and revolt in the working class. We have thus a contradiction between the interests of the masses who want to preserve and to improve their living standards and the vision of progress implemented forcibly by the decision-makers.

This contradiction underlies the outbreak of the crisis in Gierek's Poland. The ambitious plans of 'dynamic development' were supported by the masses in the expectation of a general improvement of living standards. When it became obvious that accelerated industrialisation would put heavy pressure on the population, and require many sacrifices, people refused to co-operate. Nevertheless, the government persisted in its policy, playing for time and postponing the outbreak of open crisis instead of solving it, an attitude which contributed to the worsening of the economic situation.

Pajestka is thus inclined to believe that the policy of rapid economic growth does not offer any prospects for the future. He expresses the view that the new system brought to life in 1980 allows economic strategy to be shaped by consensus and agreement and offers an answer to the apparently insoluble contradiction between the logic of economic development and the material needs of the masses.

As far as sociological explanations are concerned the emphasis shifts from economic factors to their social and political correlates, which are regarded by some sociologists as more important in generating successive crises than the economy itself. Stefan Nowak, a distinguished Polish sociologist, points out that economic disintegration was an outcome of sociological and psychological mechanisms. The breakdown of public transport or power supplies cannot be explained by economic causes only. Although the Polish crisis had some external causes, it was predominantly due to deep social conflicts (Nowak, 1981).

Referring to the cyclical nature of Polish crises, Nowak states that the whole history of post-war Poland was permeated by the ever-present discrepancy between social needs, values and aspirations on the one hand, and the activities carried out to satisfy these needs and expectations on the other. The planners and decision-makers believe that human needs should be respected, and as such these needs are taken into account in the objectives they were pursuing. Yet human needs are ignored whenever other targets conflict with them. Nowak distinguishes material needs, needs for equality and justice, and needs for democracy and freedom. He points out that socialism is usually presented as the embodiment of the ideals of equality and justice and is therefore criticised on the basis of the very ideology it tries to instil and legitimise.

As far as democracy and freedom are concerned, all public opinion surveys demonstrate that these needs are most important and when they cannot be satisfied, people withdraw to the sphere of privacy. Disintegration of independent organisations and associations leads to the growing atomisation of society. Individuals who in defiance of the general public mood are co-operating with the authorities are haunted by feelings of humiliation and isolation.

According to Nowak the system was torn by inner contradictions; the authorities were more and more concerned with maintaining and reinforcing the existing power-structures and, as a result of this, all attempts to reform the system were either ignored or actively opposed. This tendency inevitably led to further material deprivations and increased social inequality, which in turn reinforced the coercive elements of the system. Society was incapacitated, deprived of the chance to defend itself, and this powerlessness reinforced the tendency of the powerholders to ignore social needs whenever other objectives required them to do so.

There was, in other words, a constant conflict between the rulers and the ruled. The covert crisis tended to erupt into open crisis when material deprivations reached a point at which they could no longer be tolerated. Material needs proved to be less flexible in this respect than the needs for egalitarianism or democracy. The latter needs were thus usually suppressed, creating enormous pressures and tensions which erupted at crucial moments during the continuing crisis.

Thus Nowak presents a pattern of development in which latent and open crisis follow each other. This pattern was broken in Poland by the fact that the authorities were prepared to make concessions instead of resorting to coercion. As a result, a system was created in which the government and the trade unions have, for the first time, a chance to co-operate, at first on a limited scale.

Finally, one should mention a most impressive contribution to the discussion about Polish crises presented in two volumes published by Polish sociologists in Warsaw. One volume appeared in English in 1982 as an issue of a periodical published in English by the Polish Academy of Science, *Crisis and Conflicts, The Case of Poland 1980-1981*. The second volume, *Democracy and Economy*, was published in 1983 by Warsaw University in a stencilled edition under the editorship of Witold Morawski.

A central thesis with which most co-authors in both studies would certainly agree was expressed by Pánków

when he stated that the deepest roots of the crises in Poland
are to be sought in the crisis of the power structure (Pánków,
1982). In contrast to the earlier theories of alienation in
which the same thesis has been spelled out in a very general
way, the authors present a detailed analysis of many
different aspects of the Communist party–state which have
contributed to the recurring crises in Poland. The most
interesting points in that analysis could be summarised as
follows:

1) Political structure in Poland is characterised by a high
degree of internal inconsistency which results from a
development in which new forms are superimposed over the
old ones. Present-day Communist societies are characterised
by structural complexity and structural inconsistency at the
same time. Totalitarian traits permeate the policy of top
administrators, the middle ground remains the battlefield of
sectional interests, while at the bottom the cleavages
between the ruling apparati and the masses become more
and more pronounced (Rychard, 1983).

2) The institutional framework in Poland was imposed by
the Russians after the Second World War. The system,
based on Soviet patterns, has hardly evolved since then,
although after Stalin's death internal factors gained in
importance in the development and change of Polish society.

Such a system favours partiality and gives some groups in
society a much better chance of promoting their interests
than other groups who are deprived of any influence on
decision-making. The partiality is, however, hidden behind
the smokescreen of rational planning (see Kamiński, 1983,
pp.117–56).

The partiality of the economic and social policies pursued
by Communist governments itself destabilises the system;
while the expectations of the masses are ignored and their
basic needs neglected, some suffer less than others and there
are some who are able to improve their living standards even
in conditions of a deteriorating economic situation.

3) The defects of centralised planning consist not only in
unfair redistribution of economic benefits through decisions
which favour some interests while neglecting others, but also
of erroneous or ineffective strategies.

Central planning favours accelerated economic growth which suppresses all other social objectives. Excessive investment invariably leads to reductions of output in sectors which provide consumer goods and services. Instead of satisfying the expectations and aspirations of the population, central planning gives production an overwhelming priority over consumption, which affects the living standards of the masses.

4) Centralised planning is characterised by its own 'pathology', which has been represented by Barbara Błaszczyk as follows: (a) the atrophy of the strategic functions of planning; (b) neglect of social objectives in economic planning; (c) dealing in a deterministic way with social processes which are by their very nature probabilistic; (d) too detailed and pervasive planning; (e) inadequate information underlying planning decisions and (f) the illusory character of the central plan (Błaszczyk, 1983, p.182).

The deficiencies of centralised planning are so serious that even the relatively privileged groups might be affected by an ailing economy (Staniszkis, 1983, p.332).

5) Why, in spite of all its shortcomings, is ineffective, 'non-dialectical' planning tolerated and even supported by the authorities? As Kamiński points out the answer is to be sought in the vested interests of the state; the doctrine of centralised planning justifies ideologically the uncontrolled power of the state (Kamiński, 1983, p.151).

The main divisions and conflicts are based on differences due to the power structure: the administrators of social, political and economic life constitute a group distinguished by their political domination and economic privilege, while other groups, referred to by Rychard (1983) as the class of labour and by Kurczewski (1982) as the middle class, are more and more frustrated because their political status and economic rewards do not match their role and importance in society.

6) The predicament of the workers in such a system is particularly acute. References to excessive consumer expectations of the workers on the eve of the 1980 crisis should be dismissed as a myth used to justify the shortcomings of

the system (Widera, 1983, p.300).

7) Economic and political crises are an inevitable outcome of such a system.

The post-1945 political history of Poland can be described as a cyclical process in which the dominant apparatus of power moves towards and away from legitimacy based on public approval. That process, in a system which directly combines political and economic power, coincides with a process of cyclical economic ups and downs. (Kurczewski, 1982, p.29). By participating in the successive crises in their recent history, the Polish people have to come to the conclusion that the bureaucratic structures, and the system of power behind them, are incapable of changing their policies without social pressure exerted upon them,

explains W. Morawski (1981, p17).

The views we have discussed exemplify considerable differences in the level of generalisation on which the causes of Polish crises are tackled. Some explanations focus on wrong strategies, others reveal pathological aspects in the development of Polish political structure attributed either to the influence of the Russians or the narrow interests of the ruling bureaucracies. The most comprehensive explanations focus on the systemic features of Communist societies, and go far beyond the conventional arguments provided by the reports sponsored by the party (see Kubiak, 1982).

None of these explanations, however, answers a simple question: why, of all Communist countries, has Poland been the only country in which crises have occurred with striking regularity? All Communist countries were subject to the same mechanisms of selection of political leaders, so why should Polish leaders be more prone to make mistakes in their policies? All Communist countries have the same economic and political institutions which give no room for the representation of group interests and deny the workers the right of political decision-making, yet only in Poland has this led to the outbreak of social rebellion. And if Communist economies are basically unable to give people what they want, why are some East European countries doing economically much better than Poland?

The answer can at least be partly sought in the specific nature of Polish society, its tradition, political culture, ideological myths, long-established relationships with its neighbours and the memories of past conflicts and disputes.

In most Western studies of Poland all these factors have been thoroughly and convincingly accounted for, as in, for example, the important works by Leslie *et al.*, (1980), Dziewanowski (1977), and Davis (1981).

There is no doubt that the historical heritage weighs heavily on Poland's development and determines much of what has happened since the Communists came to power. Yet there are reasons to believe that post-1944 factors might have influenced Poland's fate as well. There are, after all, many converging patterns in the development of Poland and other East European countries in spite of differences in their pre-war history. Would there be other patterns of divergence attributable to post-war development? And if there are, what role do they play in making Poland so much more vulnerable economically and politically? (See: Weydenthal 1978, 1979a; Ascherson, 1981; and Ash, 1983.)

How and when did Poland embark on the course which ended with the turmoil of 1980? Should we start with 1944, when Poland found herself in the orbit of Russian influence, or in 1948, when the process of Stalinist unification was intensified, or with the post-Stalinist period of 1954–6 when the enforced sovietisation of Eastern Europe was relaxed?

One evident truth is that the development of the countries of Eastern Europe in the years 1945–53 was increasingly convergent. The year 1948 was a turning point in many respects but its main importance lay in the enforcement of the 'Stalinisation' and sovietisation of Eastern Europe.

The first crisis followed Stalin's death and the struggle for succession. What happened in Poland at that time was, as we shall see, an integral part of the post-Stalinist crisis in the Soviet empire.

The second crisis in Poland signed the death warrant of Gomułka's regime. It took place in 1968, but came to a head in 1970, when Gomułka was removed and replaced by Gierek. The crisis of 1968 marked the bankruptcy of post-October economic and social policy. It reflected the bitter power struggle within the ruling élite.

The third stage of crises in Poland covers the years

1970–81, and can be regarded as the opening of a new stage in the political struggle in which the authorities are directly challenged by a defiant mass movement of the workers.

THE CONVERGING PATTERNS OF CHANGE IN EAST EUROPEAN SOCIETIES AFTER THE SECOND WORLD WAR

There is no doubt that by the end of the war the situation in East European countries varied greatly from one country to another. While Yugoslavia enjoyed full independence, Hungary and Rumania were under direct Soviet control, which allowed local Communist governments to establish themselves. East Germany, deprived of the status of an autonomous state, was under the direct rule of the Soviet military forces. Czechoslovakia and Poland were formally independent and in spite of the presence of the Soviet army political institutions retained the appearance of full sovereignty.

In spite of the differences, there was one common denominator which determined the fate of all East European countries after 1945: *the power and influence of the Soviet Union, recognised by international agreements which, in fact, if not in the letter, granted Stalin a free hand in this part of Europe.*

In Poland communist rule was inextricably associated with the Soviet regime which excited considerable resentment (see Kersten, 1982). This owed much to past history but, more importantly, memories were still fresh of the Russo-German pact of 1939, of tens of thousands of Poles dragged to labour camps, of Katyń, of the ruthless extermination of the Home Army troops in the Eastern parts of Poland in 1944, of the lack of support for the Warsaw uprising, of the loss of Lwów and Wilno, and the uprooting of millions of people from eastern Poland. Moreover, Poland was the only country in the Russian zone which had come out of the war with a powerful underground movement, developed during the war under the leadership of the Polish government-in-exile in London. The Home Army had been largely swept away in the Warsaw uprising, but the number of their remaining forces was still considerable, and its prestige among the Poles was very high. The government-in-exile was generally respected as the country's legitimate ruling body. The Church retained spiritual leadership as the living symbol of national continuity and independence.

The programme offered by the Communists focused on issues acceptable to the overwhelming majority. Land reform, nationalisation of industry, democratisation of education, extensive settlement in the western regions taken from the Germans and the economic reconstruction of the country after the destructive effects of war, were targets which secured the co-operation of the Polish people with the government in its attempts to reach those targets. What was lacking was direct or indirect consensus about the Communist takeover, but in Poland, and in other East European countries, the Soviet army was the dominant force, able to give full support to the Communist power structures.

The first Polish government created under the Soviet umbrella presented itself as a government based on a coalition of democratic parties, but for the majority of observers it was obvious that this was but a passing phase with the balance of forces heavily in favour of open Communist dictatorship.

Although the practicalities of the ascent to power by Communist parties varied in Eastern Europe from one country to another according to circumstances, in all these countries the fundamental Communist strategy was becoming strikingly familiar. It consisted in (a) crushing pockets of armed resistance; (b) eliminating the political forces which openly resisted the Communists; (c) dislodging the allied parties which were opposed to the further extension of Communist hegemony; (d) breaking the tendency of the socialist movement to retain its own identity and independence from the Communist leadership, and eventually (e) purging the Communist elements resisting the outright sovietisation of the East European countries.

Many Communist ideologists try to present Gomułka's reign in Poland in 1945–8 as a moderate, open and responsive form of socialism, but if we rightly contrast

Gomułka's relatively liberal post-war policy with the Stalinist rule which followed his fall, one cannot fail to see at the same time the ruthless struggle for power carried out by Gomułka and his party in the years 1945–8 (see Kersten, 1982). Up to 1947 fighting went on with armed groups operating in southern Poland and defying the new government. Mikołajczyk became the target of an uncompromising political campaign which ended with a massive electoral fraud. The 'new' i.e., heavily purged and restructured Polish Socialist Party was compelled to endorse the idea of unification with the Communist Party (Polish Workers' Party by that time) and the security forces filled the prisons with political prisoners in an attempt to eradicate all forms of organised political opposition.

Thus we come to the inevitable conclusion that Polish Communists did not have a chance of deviating from the Stalinist pattern of development, once the anti-Communist resistance within the country was broken, the allied parties firmly under control, and the socialists 'united' under the leadership of their Communist colleagues. Hence the argument of some Polish scholars, that the events of 1948 were decisive in generating the gap between the rulers and the ruled, can be seen as an attempt to put all the blame on Stalin and his supporters within the ranks of Polish Communists.

To summarise: up to 1947 the East European societies within the Soviet sphere of influence moved partly along their own trajectories but there is no doubt that there was a growing convergence of the patterns they followed.

As we have indicated, the decisive underlying factor which determined that development was the domination of the USSR over Eastern Europe. There was no reason for snubbing the offer of the Marshall Plan, calling for collectivisation of the Soviet type and raising a witch-hunt against the traitors and cosmopolites among the highest Communist ranks other than the Stalinist policy of sovietisation of Eastern Europe and reinforcement of the grip of the USSR over the satellite countries.

The years 1949–54 marked a new stage usually described as the sovietisation of Eastern Europe. The main changes which took place, at an amazingly accelerated rate in those years, included: (a) the remodelling of political institutions in line with the Soviet pattern of the party–state; (b) the establishment of the direct rule of the secret police; (c) the policy of mass terror and purges based on bogus accusations against imperialist spies and traitors within the ranks of the party leadership; (d) the setting up of a new economic programme of industrialisation and full-scale collectivisation; (e) a cultural revolution aimed at a totally uniform culture and the intensive indoctrination of the younger generation; (f) an uncompromising struggle against the Catholic Church, and (g) the reinforcement of direct supervision of the state and party organs by Russian officials and advisers.

A high degree of convergence of social and political change in eastern Europe in those years was thus based on the direct imposition of the Soviet model of government, economy and society. Attempts to defend national traditions and institutions were regarded with suspicion, while the Soviet style of life was proclaimed as the most advanced expression of socialist development.

In such a system coercion was indispensable to suppress the underlying political and national conflict between the Stalinist governments and East European societies. The harsh economic realities of accelerated growth, combined with the rule of terror and offensive against the national traditions and cultural heritage generated deep social tensions and widened the gap between the rulers and the ruled.

It follows that the political crisis which erupted in East Europe after Stalin's death has to be assessed on its own terms even if many ingredients of that crisis will reappear in crises generated by other circumstances.

THE CRISIS IN EASTERN EUROPE 1954–1956 AND ITS DIVERGING EFFECTS

The struggle for succession in the USSR which followed Stalin's death, and the changes which took place in Eastern

Europe can be separated into three successive stages: (a) the Malenkov–Beria interregnum; (b) the Krushchev anti-Stalinist crusade and the reform movement in Eastern Europe; culminating in (c) the invasion of Hungary and the victory of the Polish October (see Sakwa, 1978).

The first attempt at the revision of Stalinist policy by the competing factions in the USSR took place at a time when, in Eastern Europe, Stalinist transformations were accelerated. The people's democracies were going through the most difficult period of rapid industrialisation, enforced collectivisation was in full swing, show trials were organised on massive scale, the oppressive force of the secret police was increasing, and living standards were rapidly deteriorating.

The 'little Stalins' in Eastern Europe were thus faced with an unexpected and most embarrassing U-turn initiated by their Soviet masters who preached the necessity of a new economic policy. Yet the established leaders in Eastern Europe seemed determined to continue their line, even if they had to ignore the signs coming from the Kremlin.

Beria's removal and Malenkov's dismissal opened a new period in the power struggle in the Kremlin: Krushchev and his supporters were now faced with the hard-core Stalinist faction, headed by Molotov and Kaganovich. It was only by extending his criticism of Stalinist policies that Krushchev could improve his position and win support among the Soviet bureaucracy eager to get rid of the fear, insecurity and harsh discipline imposed by Stalin.

On the European scene, the new line pursued by Krushchev brought *rapprochement* with Tito. The joint declaration in Belgrade of 3 June 1955, declared Yugoslavia's Communism acceptable to the Soviet bloc, and cast doubt on the validity of previous accusations of the nationalist-rightist deviation, directed against the Yugoslavian leaders. The trials of Rajk in Hungary, Kostov in Bulgaria, and the campaign against Gomułka in Poland, all linked with the fight against Titoism, were thus directly brought into question.

The reactions of the 'little Stalins' heading the East European parties varied from country to country, according to the local situation.

Where 'little Stalins' and their factions felt their power directly threatened by the new policy, they stopped expecting any help from Moscow and looked for alternatives. Gheorgiu-Dej in Rumania and Hodja in Albania made their first overtures to China, seeing in Mao an ally in their fight for the preservation of the Stalinist order.

Where the leaders felt relatively secure and enjoyed the support of the new Soviet leadership, they played down the changes and dealt harshly with liberal opposition. In East Germany, Ulbricht declared that since no show trials were promoted by the party, the leadership had nothing to revise. At the same time, Ulbricht carried out important modifications in his economic policy, and took the first steps towards *rapprochement* with West Germany—a policy which was to bring real benefits in the future.

In Poland and Hungary the situation was more complicated. The response to the reformist overtures signalled from Moscow split the party ranks and activated political divisions among the ruling political élites. The denouncement of Beria (and understandably his local henchmen) caused havoc among the party rank and file, while the growing conflict at the top between hard-liners and moderates of the party offered the reformers a chance to speak their minds in public.

In both Poland and Hungary one can distinguish similar trends:

1) The literary journals gave the lead to 'revisionist' ideas (see Fejtö, 1971): *Nowa Kultura* and *Przeglad Kulturalny* in Poland, and *Irodalmi Ujsag* in Hungary, enjoyed great popularity and brought the most unorthodox ideas to the public, such as the famous 'Poem for Adults' by Adam Ważyk in Poland, to give just one example.

2) Daily newspapers also played their part in the general intellectual and political ferment. Fejtö notes that, between 1954 and 1956, Rákosi had to replace forty-six of the fifty-two staff members of the official party organ, *Szabad Nép*. In Poland, the daily *Życie Warszawy* played a similar role.

3) Party organisations in higher schools and universities were also in a state of uproar and permanent discussion, and

became nuclei for the spread of dissent to other political and intellectual centres.

4) In 1956, clubs for discussion were mushrooming all over Hungary and Poland. In Hungary the Petöfi Club was the most influential: in some of the discussion meetings thousands participated. In Poland, the 'Klub Krzywego Koła' played a similar role, while many other discussion centres started up in the provinces.

5) In both countries young people, formerly activists in the youth organisations, and members of the party were most active in demanding and struggling for reforms. In Poland, a publication for young people, the weekly *Po Prostu*, was certainly instrumental in stirring up a mass movement, both among the young intelligentsia and in some working-class centres.

The differences between Poland and Hungary were, however, considerable. In Hungary, the Stalinist old guard was well entrenched in positions in the leadership, and this explains why Krushchev did not support any direct measures against Hungarian liberals, and even tacitly supported the reform movement when they demanded the rehabilitation of Laszlo Rajk, and the condemnation of show trials.

Rákosi decided to call a Central Committee meeting in order to mobilise his supporters, expel his radical opponents, and close the Petöfi Club. There were even plans to arrest the dissenters and to close their newspapers. In the circumstances Mikoyan and Suslov intervened: they came to Budapest to enforce Rákosi's resignation. Rákosi was replaced by a moderate Stalinist Gerö, but this change infuriated both the hard-liners and the radicals.

A political vacuum followed, because Imre Nagy did not seem prepared to give a lead to the reform movement, and the focus of this movement shifted away from the ranks of the party. A short-lived revolution met with a tragic end with the Russian intervention and considerable bloodshed.

In Poland, the situation developed in a different way. The Central Committee was divided here too, but following Bierut's death it was the centrists and moderates who held positions of power, and looked for the support of the dissenters and rebels among the party rank and file against their hard-line opponents. In their final battle against the so-called 'Natolin' group (supported by that time by the USSR) they called for Gomułka to step in. In contrast to Nagy, Gomułka did not hesitate to take the lead. From the very start, he stubbornly refused to accept any post other than that of a First Secretary. For Poles, he was a symbol of resistance to Stalinism and, once elevated to the leadership position, he was able to carry out substantial reforms under the guidance of the party and prevent the mass movement from getting out of hand.

As we see, the political crises in Poland and Hungary began as crises of the establishment. The succession struggle in the USSR and the subsequent split among the party leadership created a situation in which the coercive power of the state seemed to be paralysed. It should be recalled that the early outbreaks of mass protest after Stalin's death—in Czechoslovakia in May 1953 and in Germany in June 1953 were brutally suppressed. And so was the workers' rebellion in Poland in June 1956, but by that time the authorities were no longer able to control the course of events and the repressions against the workers mobilised a mass movement all over Poland and strengthened the hand of the reformers within the party leadership.

It should be further noted that the mass movement was directed in its early stage against Stalinist policies which gave the party in Poland the chance to channel it into a framework of reformism controlled by the moderate and revisionist groups within the party.

And finally the crisis occurred at the early stage of accelerated industrialisation when the redistribution of national resources gave the chance of rapid improvement in the living standards of the population: the new economic policy effectively helped to defuse mass discontent.

Following the development of political events after Stalin's death considerable differences between East European countries emerged. Some countries remained frozen in their Stalinist forms, others adopted a new post-Stalinist version of Soviet Communism, while Poland emerged from the turmoil as the only country in which vital elements of the Soviet model of Communism have been discarded.

Reforms carried out in Poland in the years 1956–8 helped in the short term to re-establish some sort of social and political stability, but did not guarantee such stability in the future. There was an obvious dichotomy between the many liberal reforms carried out during the period of political upheaval, and the real power structure in which the party–state apparatus and the coercive organs of the state played the dominant and decisive role.

There were also never-ending squabbles between the state apparatus and the party apparatus, which felt threatened by Gomułka's policy. The party was far from being united, since the hard-liners felt that they had strong support within the Communist bloc, and were waiting for the opportunity to recover full control of the situation. Gomułka himself was torn between the pressure of the party–state bureaucracy and the demands of a mixed economy which required maximum flexibility and genuine incentives. The reforms were difficult to digest, and attempts to undermine them started as soon as Gomułka established his rule. Many of these reforms, however, such as private agriculture and the concessions made to the Church, were to stay, and posed by themselves new problems for the party–state apparatus.

We can conclude that the aftermath of the Polish October was a situation in which a number of factors combined to prevent lasting stability. Poland was to become the 'sick man' of Eastern Europe; the crisis of 1968 appears as some sort of natural continuation of the processes which occurred in 1955–6 in Poland.

1968—A CRISIS OF GOMUŁKA'S POST-OCTOBER ESTABLISHMENT

The period of consolidation and stabilisation enjoyed by Gomułka's regime was of relatively short duration. The logic of economic development soon took its toll. The increase in food prices in 1959 and 1965 were unpopular, and were hardly able to maintain the balance of the market, in view of the widening gap between the burden of investments and the supply of consumer goods. The technocrats were disillusioned in view of Gomułka's resistance to the launching of a wider programme of economic reconstruction. The party ideological apparatus felt redundant because of the pragmatism of the ruling élite and their insensitivity to the educational and propaganda value of Marxist dogma. The managers resented the crippling bureaucratic strait-jacket of economic administration, and the party zealots within the state apparatus were disillusioned by what they regarded as a lack of opportunities for promotion based on political criteria.

The feeling of economic stalemate and frustration which dominated Poland in the mid-sixties helped to stir up discontent directed against the party leadership. The reshuffle in the secret police, and the promotion of General Moczar to Minister of Internal Affairs opened up to his faction of so-called 'partisans' a genuine prospect of victory in the power struggle.

The members of the secret political police, the army and militia men, the party apparatus, many officials who saw in the support of the party new opportunities for their careers, and many unsuccessful contenders for high prestige jobs, regarded the Moczar movement as the chance of their life. For others, it was just a way of breaking the mould, caused, they believed, by the lack of effective leadership. And there were many members of the party and state apparatus who felt attracted by the ideology professed by Moczar's faction with its strong nationalism, veiled anti-Russian sentiments and clear anti-Semitic undertones. Moczar did not hesitate to represent the liberal intelligentsia within the party ranks as the vanguard of the Jewish conspiracy, infiltrating Poland with anti-national cosmopolitan values. His followers, many of whom belonged before the war to active fascist and anti-Semitic groups, supplied the Moczar faction with time-worn clichés about Jews whose infiltration into Polish political, cultural and intellectual life had to be stopped once and for ever. The anti-Semitic theme was brought into the open and converted into a major issue of the partisans' crusade after the 1967 Israeli-Arab war, when it became possible to accuse some of the centrist or moderate members of the establishment of Jewish origin of allegedly favouring

Israel and betraying the national interests of socialist Poland.

The end of 1967 and the beginning of 1968 brought, however, a new element to the political scene in Poland. The growth of the democratic movement among students, the hopes of the liberals at developments in Czechoslovakia, the decay in the cohesiveness of the Soviet bloc due to the open dissent of Rumania, all played a part. In 1968 Russian dissidents voiced their criticism of the totalitarian regime and in the spring of 1968 the pace of the democratic awakening in Czechoslovakia quickened.

Despite this, the anti-liberal forces in Poland were on the offensive. The defeat of the student movement in March 1968, the mass arrests of students and young university dons who participated in the demonstrations, the vilification campaign against the few intellectuals who supported the young rebels, mass purges of people of Jewish origin (publicly justified by the necessity to have the country free from the Zionist plot) and similar purges of all those Gentiles who dared to oppose this policy, created in Poland a new situation and opened the way to a massive attack on institutions established in post-October Poland, brought a reshuffle of the cadres and extended the control of the political police over all spheres of social life.

In the course of this action, the party apparatus recovered the ground it lost in the previous decade, party secretaries interfered in all decisions of the state organs, professional bodies were deprived of the autonomy they enjoyed and there followed a general promotion to positions of importance and influence of party hacks and active supporters of the purge.

As a result of the changes, the party underwent a process of uniformity which would have seemed unthinkable a few years earlier. The political line of the hard-liners was victorious, dissent was eradicated, conformity reinforced, blind discipline restored, and the selection of the political riff-raff to positions of power and influence virtually institutionalised.

The main outcome of the 1968 crisis in Poland was a total clamp-down on the democratic opposition. The changes implemented after 1968 brought Poland in line with other East European countries which had never undergone the process of post-Stalinist liberal reforms. The Polish October was solidly buried, the party apparatus reinforced and the secret police reinstated as the watchdog of political loyalty. In this respect Poland and Czechoslovakia paradoxically shared the same fate in 1968, with this one important difference. In Czechoslovakia the intervention stabilised the power of the authoritarian leadership, while in Poland the success of the crusade against the rebellious students and of the anti-liberal purges left the crisis within the ruling élite unresolved. This was in contrast to other countries in the Communist bloc where the peculiar brand of sovietisation was either never challenged or safely re-established and where the élite operated according to a well-known and legitimised formula. Gomułka, who maintained his power thanks to the direct interference of Russia, was completely isolated. The party apparatus was openly hostile to the old man, the liberals whom he used to play off against the hard-liners in the Central Committee and government had been purged, and the position of his closest supporters was undermined. It was obvious to everybody that his victory over his rivals was only temporary and his former supporters and clients were looking elsewhere to secure their political future. At a time when economic reforms· were badly needed, economic growth slowed down and the imbalance in the market grew—a phenomenon apparent in the acute shortages of basic food products. The country was faced with a precarious situation with the choice between the isolated and discredited leader, and his rapacious rivals among whom the head of the political police was the leading figure.

After 1968, economic and social objectives did not change, the only meaningful addition to political thought being the witch-hunt against 'revisionists' and the vulgar anti-Semitism preached by the party propaganda apparatus. Converts to the new party line had to absorb this package to prove that they could be trusted as party zealots. This was a situation which alienated many people and left room for cynics, careerists, simpletons and *sui generis* fascists who welcomed the revival of authoritarianism and full-scale anti-Semitism in the party.

Reforms put forward by Gomułka in 1970 required public support because they contained a package of price rises and wage restraints which brought new hardships and an inevitable lowering of living standards for a while at least. Support was lacking, however, both from the party–state bureaucracy and from the workers who faced years of economic scarcity and felt deceived by the party leadership. Faced with an officially announced fall in living standards by about 2 per cent (according to realistic estimates more like 7 per cent) the workers responded with mass riots.

On the bloody Thursday of 17th December 1970, Gomułka decided to use force to suppress the protest. Hundreds of people were wounded and killed and, amid general shock and horror, the old man was singled out by his comrades as solely responsible for these events, and had to go.

The workers' revolt of 1970 brought about a new equipe and paved the way for new policies, which seemed at first to be a response to the problems of the ailing Polish economy. The irony of history lay in the repetition of the pattern in which initial reforms and changes were followed by a retreat from the pledges of the new leadership and the explosive confrontations of 1976 and 1980 which put an end to Gierek's regime.

CONCLUSIONS

Our outline of the course of events up to the nineteen-seventies would suggest that up to 1953–4 Eastern Europe was subject to a process of progressive uniformisation which reflected and implemented Stalin's plan of far-reaching and accelerating integration of the Soviet empire. To quote T. G. Ash:

It is sometimes suggested that the Sovietisation of Poland only began in earnest with the American declaration of Cold War in late 1946. The reverse is nearer to the truth: the Cold War was, in part, a western response to the Sovietisation of Poland which began when the first NKVD man set foot on Polish soil. (Ash, 1983, p.5)

There seems to be no doubt that as long as the Stalinist model was in force any changes from within were unlikely: in that sense the petrification theory would be revindicated. It is at the same time true that for various reasons the ruling political élites had sooner or later to modify the political system and adopt an authoritarian power structure better suited to the processes of advanced industrialisation and conflict management.

The adjustment took place amidst a political crisis which occurred after Stalin's death and affected many countries at once; a situation which was never to be repeated again. The outcome of that crisis was also unique: Albania and Rumania were able to reaffirm their independence from the USSR while Poland embarked on a course of economic and political reforms which made it a society quite different from her Communist neighbours.

The crisis which developed in the late nineteen-sixties in Czechoslovakia revealed many characteristics of the 1956 crises: it was an attempt to shake up Stalinist institutions and was generated, as in Poland in 1956, by the revisionists within the party.

The crisis in 1968 in Poland marked in that respect a completely different pattern; its character supports the arguments of those who warn against the over-generalisations about the causes of Communist crises. On the one hand, that crisis reflected the new aspirations developed after 1954–6 which the party failed to satisfy. On the other hand, these aspirations were exploited in the factional struggle within the party in which the most militant factions tried to turn the clock back and eradicate all major concessions of the previous period. The fact that they did not achieve a complete victory was, however, of great importance as far as further political developments were concerned. The badly needed economic reform of supply prices combined with drastic consumer price rises and wage restraint could not succeed in conditions where the power structure was weakened by factional squabbles and mutual accusations which were undermining the credibility of the party leadership.

Bearing in mind the history of Eastern Europe after 1956

one could conclude that an authoritarian power structure has to rely heavily on naked power if the state is to carry out its functions of centralised economic management. The 'modernisation' of the political regimes does not imply therefore any weakening of the coercion built into them.

Whether Communist authoritarianism must be less stable than the Stalinist model is another matter. Bearing in mind recurrent crises in Poland some observers draw the far-fetched conclusion that this is indeed the case. Some are even inclined to believe that there is some sort of cyclical development of Communist economy and polity and see in it a direct analogy with the capitalist 'crises' which for many decades occurred in the West with striking regularity.

Such a conclusion is based on the tendency to replace historical explanations by sociological ones, that is to see in historical processes the manifestations of general social laws rather than the outcome of the special configurations and series of events which determine the differences between varying patterns of development of different countries, even if the same general laws operate in the background.

In the case of Poland the systemic explanation of the crisis does not help us to understand why Poland should experience recurring crises while other countries with similar economic and political structures did not. Even a sketchy summary of the history of political crises in Poland suggests that the crises in Poland cannot be directly explained by the cyclical development of the Polish economy, by class conflict, or by an inadequate institutional framework although all these factors remain in the background as the conditioning forces of political events.

3 Command economy without coercion?

THE LOGIC OF SELF-CONSUMING GROWTH

In the nineteen-seventies most Communist countries in Eastern Europe opted for the policy of accelerated economic growth oriented towards the 'bread-and-butter' economy, that is, a considerable improvement of living standards. To quote Kadar, who was one of the most ardent advocates of this development: 'The important thing is that we should have more to eat—good goulash—schools—housing and ballet' (*New York Times*, 2 April 1964).

The new policy opened a fourth period in the economic strategy pursued in Eastern Europe; the first one was characterised by the post-war reconstruction of the economy; during the second (1949–53) accelerated industrialisation was accompanied by suppressed inflation and rapidly falling living standards; Stalin's death in 1953 marked the beginning of the third period (1954–70) when a programme emerged of moderate modernisation combined with the tendency to maintain a market equilibrium by matching overall demand and supply (see Wellisz, 1964, p.85); during the fourth period, a dash for growth based on external resources aiming at the establishment of the consumer society was the dominant trend (Kusin, 1980).

The new policy assumed that accelerated development would be based on Western know-how and Western loans. The main problem for the planners consisted in achieving this without overheating the economy, but could this target be successfully implemented within the framework of command economy?

It should be noted that a theory of socialist economy developed in the nineteen-thirties emphasised the necessity of market mechanisms if the economy were to be efficient (Taylor and Lange, 1938). Although the theory of market socialism was regarded for a long time as an unpardonable

55

deviation from Communist doctrine, many East European economists would at present agree that the severe distortions of economic equilibrium in their countries must be attributed to centralised economic management and the limited role of competition and the market mechanisms.

The nature of these distortions has been widely discussed in connection with the recurring crises in Communist economies (see Markus, 1981). Economists are inclined to believe that there are several factors which contribute to the cyclical perturbations of economic balance, the most important being: a) priority given to heavy industry; b) enforcement of the maximal rate of growth; and c) taut bureaucratic planning.

All these factors have been found in the background of the economic imbalances which plagued Communist societies: they loomed in the mid-fifties when the Stalinist pattern of industrialisation caused a rapid deterioration of living standards in all East European countries. They were visible in Czechoslovakia in 1967 (see Korda, 1976), and their influence accounted, according to many economists, for the outbreak of economic crises in Poland in 1970 and 1980.

In the introduction of a report presented to the Polish leadership by a group of economists, headed by Gościński, we read:

The enforcement of a maximal rate of growth is, in a way, a built-in tendency of the political authorities. A climate of fascination with the high rate of growth of the national income and the global product operated in this direction. In such a spirit and in such terms we measured and expressed our success in catching up with the most developed countries. It is a kind of overheating of the booming economy under socialism. (Gościński, 26 February 1981)

The economists argue that these processes bring about unavoidable cyclical crises. The report prepared by Gościński and his associates points out that the cyclical development of the command economy goes through three basic stages. (This view is also propounded by Korda (1976) who examined development in Czechoslovakia before 1968).

1) Stage one: take-off of growth and first successes in the implementation of the tout plans.
2) Stage two: first difficulties due to limited resources (labour force, raw materials, imports, etc.) which lead to more or less constant imbalance of the market supplying both the producer and consumer, and increased inflation. The net effects of this development are the breakdown of investment projects (frozen investments), deterioration of the discipline of work and inflationary pay rises.
3) Stage three: a revision of the planned objectives becomes unavoidable, cuts are made in investments, raw materials, foreign-currency expenditure, wages and employment. These cuts generate social tensions (see also Mieczkowski, 1979)

There is no doubt that the sequence described by Gościński and his associates characterises all Communist societies in which economy is based on the principle of centralised management. It should be noted, however, that the imbalances caused by this pattern of development vary in scope from one country to another. It seems that the impact of the imbalances generated by the command economy will depend to a great extent on the measures undertaken by governments and the stage when readjustments become necessary.

In our survey of the Gomułka period, we have pointed to the economic difficulties which were felt in the last years of his rule but there are reasons to believe that if they had been dealt with the way Gomułka planned there would have been no crisis of the kind experienced in Poland in 1980. This would suggest that the cyclical development of Communist economies and cyclical increases of social tensions associated with it do not necessitate the outbreak of economic and political crises.

Whether a revision of the planned objectives succeeds or not and the social conflicts reach the critical point depends on some other conditions which have not been accounted for.

Moreover, variation over time in the growth rate of investment and of real wages does not reveal a clear pattern of cycles of the kind described above. Stanisław Gomułka

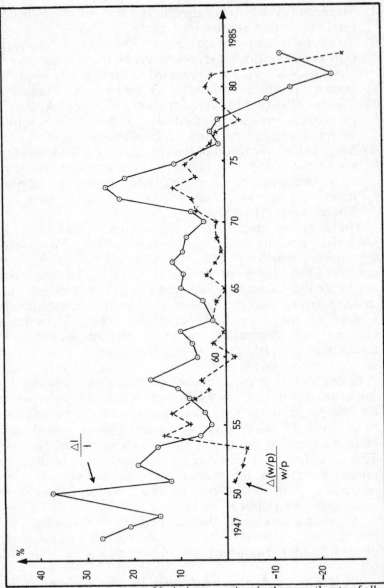

Figure 3·1: Polish economy. Variation over time in the growth rate of all investment in fixed capital assets, △ I/I, and in the growth rate of real wages in the socialised sector, △ (w/p)/(w/p) (Stanislaw Gomułka).

(1984a) points in his study to the fact that the relationship between investments and incomes was determined by many different factors affecting the decisions of the central planners. A graph prepared by S. Gomułka to support this argument in my study reveals a striking difference between the cautious policy of Władysław Gomułka and the adventurous pattern of investments in the periods which preceded and followed his rule.

CROSS-NATIONAL COMPARISONS

Looking at the economic development of East European countries in the nineteen-seventies, the similarity of the economic policies pursued can easily be noticed. Let us have a look at the general performance of the East European countries measured by their industrial output.

Table 3·1 Annual growth rates of gross industrial production of CMEA states, 1971-9 (in per cent)

	1971-5	1976-80	1976-8	1976	1977	1978	1979
Bulgaria	9.1	9.0	6.8	6.8	6.8	6.9	6.5
Czechoslovakia	6.7	5.3	6.2	6.5	5.6	5.0	3.7
GDR	6.5	6.8–7.2	5.1	5.9	4.8	4.7	4.8
Hungary	6.4	6.7–7.0	5.5	4.1	6.8	5.2	2.8
Poland	10.4	8.5	7.0	9.3	7.5	4.8	2.8
Rumania	12.9	10.7	11.1	11.4	12.5	9.0	8.0
USSR	7.4	7.0–7.8	5.1	4.8	5.7	4.8	3.4

Source: Kux (1980) p.28.

It should be noted that all East European countries relied heavily during that time on foreign loans. By the end of the decade they were all left with a considerable foreign debt; their indebtedness to the West has grown from 6.5 billion dollars in 1970 to 29 billion in 1975 and over 65 billion in 1979. In 1979 Poland's debt was the highest in absolute figures, but she occupied third place with regard to the debt per head.

Table 3·2 Debts per head and in relation to exports in selected East European countries, 1979

Country	Debts per head in US$	Debts as a proportion of the value of exported goods
Poland	534	3.09
Hungary	664	2.18
East Germany	549	1.92
Bulgaria	385	1.67

Sources: Fallenbuchl (1980)

It should be noted that during the nineteen-seventies the East European countries underwent a substantial modernisation of their traditional industries. However, the development of the most advanced branches, such as micro-electronics, telecommunications, computer hardware and software, etc., remained poor. Moreover, they found it difficult to compete in Western markets for traditional manufacturing goods and these difficulties became aggravated at a time of economic recession.

In spite of the many similarities in their development and economic strategies there seem to be serious differences in the way the East European countries coped with the problem posed by the fast economic growth of the nineteen-seventies. Table 3·3 deals with the crucial issue of inflation and price level in these countries.

Table 3·3 Official price index for consumer goods and foodstuffs in selected countries, 1978

	1970=100	
	Consumer goods	Foodstuffs
GDR	96.3	99.7
Bulgaria	102.8	104.7
Czechoslovakia	104.6	104.1
Hungary	130.8	132.1
Poland	134.1	136.8
Rumania	105.4	108.1
USSR	100.7	101.9

Source: International Labour Organisation (1980), p. 542.

The countries in this table can be divided into three groups. Poland and Hungary show already in 1978 a substantial rise in prices in comparison with 1970. Later on there were in these two countries even steeper price rises. Czechoslovakia and Rumania also experienced in the later nineteen-seventies considerable economic difficulties which were reflected in shortages of consumer goods (Kusin, 1982), but in 1978 the level of consumer prices was only slightly higher than in 1970. In the GDR the prices even fell slightly, in the USSR they remained about steady, and in Bulgaria there was a slight rise. Also later on there was no noticeable price rise in these three countries, though they sometimes had to deal with their difficulties in quite a drastic manner (Asmus, 1982).

One should add that the listed indices do not reflect black-market prices. These are important in a discussion of social inequality and political tensions.

The figures show that in 1978 both Poland and Hungary experienced similar effects of the overheating of the economy on consumer prices, though the Hungarian economy does not fall into the category of a fully-fledged command economy. On the other hand, other command economies did not display in 1978 the inflationary pressures faced by Poland and Hungary. Furthermore, it should be added that when the Rumanian economy went into a deep crisis in the early nineteen-eighties which necessitated steep price rises, there was in Rumania no political upheaval comparable to the Polish one.

As we see, a simple formula according to which command economy brings about cyclical economic and political crises cannot be applied. It follows that a more detailed analysis of the economic history of Poland in the nineteen-seventies will be needed. Such an analysis will help us to specify the factors which contributed to the recurrence of economic crises in Poland and which did not appear elsewhere (see Brus, 1983b).

SQUARING THE CIRCLE

Pełczyński (1982) in his study of the Polish crisis presents development in Poland after 1956 as a 'road from Communism' pointing to the role of the private sector, the elements of political pluralism and the erosion of the official ideology. Indeed, the influence of these factors can be clearly observed in Poland (see Cieplak, 1974). In fact we suggest that many of the difficulties experienced by the Polish leadership in the nineteen-seventies can be traced to the differences between Poland and the other Communist countries which arose after 1956. There is no doubt that the Polish situation in the post-Stalin years constituted a serious deviation from the Soviet model of Communism.

First, an essential component of pluralism in Polish public life has been the position of the Roman Catholic Church which the authorities did not dare to undermine. An important element of liberalisation after 1956 was a more open policy towards the West so that the traditionally significant influence of Western culture and Western ideas on Polish intellectuals has never been seriously challenged.

Secondly, a high degree of confidence developed among Polish workers. As we have said before, the effort to turn the clock back in 1968 succeeded temporarily in pacifying the intelligentsia, but the appeals of the authorities to the workers, asking them to help the party against the disaffected students, reassured the workers of their role in society.

In addition, the existence of a strong private sector, primarily in agriculture, created problems for the command economy which did not exist elsewhere in the Soviet bloc.

To summarise: Poland was in many respects different from other Communist societies but in spite of these differences it was locked into a system of command economy and authoritarian power structure and subject to the same pressures from the ruling bureaucracies. A peculiar combination of deviation and orthodoxy was, in Poland, bound to make the situation more explosive than elsewhere.

What Gierek tried to achieve in the nineteen-seventies was like squaring the circle, since he tried to play his game by two contradictory principles. On the one hand he was determined to preserve the Soviet-like model of the command economy, and on the other he tried to respond positively to the political and economic demands and pressures of the population in a situation which required austerity measures. His efforts were doomed in advance, but the only man who, in 1970, had probably a realistic vision of the gloomy future was Gomułka, whose fall paved Gierek's ultimately disastrous way.

The story starts in December 1970 with Gomułka's decision to increase consumer prices in order to eliminate the gap between demand and supply for consumer goods, especially in meat and meat products. This step was orthodox and conventional, but not so the workers' response to it—massive resistance of the workers to the packet of unpalatable economic measures took even the party leadership by surprise.

At this particular juncture *Poland again stepped out of line* with the rest of Communist societies in Eastern Europe, since the initial decision by Gomułka to use military force against the rioting workers was followed by a step, unprecedented in Communist states, of demoting the leader. The authorities opted thus for an alternative to violence and to the vigorous political repression which would have followed if Gomułka had stayed in office. An attempt at reconciliation took place and concessions were made to the demands of the masses. This had a decisive influence on the relationship between the rulers and the ruled throughout the following decade, especially in that the new leadership had clearly had to retreat further under working-class pressure. Not only did Gierek, immediately after being installed, go to the striking workers of the coastal cities and address them directly, but he found it necessary to blame the Gomułka team for a misguided economic policy and asked the workers for assistance.

The first policy declarations of the new leadership promising that the government would meet the needs of low-income families, and improve the living standards of the population by a revision of the 1971–5 plan, failed to satisfy public opinion. Though Gierek confirmed the economic necessity of the price rises introduced by Gomułka, and only promised a price freeze for two years, the strikes continued and spread to important industrial areas, compelling the government to make further concessions. On 15 February 1971, the price rises for meat and meat products were rescinded, the prices of industrial products reduced by about 7.5 per cent and wages and social benefits substantially increased.

Although concessions to workers' demands were not a matter of choice but of necessity once the option of severe repressions against the workers and the population was repudiated, there was an overall approval for a policy both of maintaining stable food prices and of increasing real incomes. Many economists welcomed the new strategy as superior to the austerity measures favoured by Gomułka. Some of them did it for tactical reasons to endorse the new leadership and make a virtue out of necessity, while others might have been genuine in their belief that an alternative strategy of economic development had been discovered.

A leading government economist and planner, Kazimierz Secomski, argued that the obvious failures of the past decade consisted in the fact that: 'Difficulties of development of that period mainly affected living standards. The implementation of the objectives of general economic growth was taking place at the price of limitations in real pay rises, which brought about a distortion of the fundamental proportions of economic development.' (Secomski, 1971)

The new five-year plan aimed at both an acceleration of economic growth and an increase of real incomes by 18–20 per cent. This was to be achieved by giving preference to investments in the sectors producing for the consumer market and for export. Secomski admitted that there would be an initial imbalance in the market, due to the rapid growth of purchasing power. The balance would have to be restored for the time being by imports financed by foreign loans. He assumed that these were temporary measures, and expressed the belief that the loans could be utilised for investment as well, so as to revitalise the economy. As he argued: 'If we plan to increase our national income by a certain percentage, borrowing could also increase by the same percentage.' The figure of 39 per cent growth of national income was mentioned at that time as a target for the end of the 1971-5 period.

However, the main problem of economic balance in the consumer market remained unsolved (Mieszczankowski, 1984). Accelerated modernisation did not result in an immediate abundance of consumer goods, but absorbed considerable material and human resources at the expense of the development of agriculture and the production of industrial consumer goods. It was assumed that between the years 1971–5 the rate of investment would grow by 7.3 per cent yearly with a total increase of 42 per cent. It was assumed at the same time that the purchasing power of the population would increase much more than that provided for by the cautious plan adopted in December 1970 and much in excess of the possible returns from modernisation and increased productivity (see Kisiel, 1975).

Thus, the decision to modernise the economy, in spite of imbalanced market conditions, was made possible by the ready availability of foreign credit which was earmarked for the import of investment, intermediate and consumer goods. It was also believed that the raging inflation in the West would mean that the loans would be repaid at a fraction of their original value. This encouraged further investment in fixed capital which by the end of 1975 reached the very high rate of 29.2 per cent of the annual national (material) product. Subsequently, economic difficulties multiplied and the disarray in the consumer market was more and more noticeable (Gomułka, 1983a).

One could argue that Gierek's attempts to solve Poland's economic problems were destined to fail (Kosiński and Wołoszyn, 1981; Mieszczankowski, 1984). There was no chance of increasing both consumption and investment at a high rate for a long time. The first two to three years created only the appearance of such a possibility because of the greater utilisation of existing reserves with the help of credit-financed imports. Once the reserves were exhausted, growth would slow down unless credits were increased on a much larger scale in order to sustain the initial success. The latter course was adopted (Gomułka, 1983a). The turning-point came after 1973 when the volume of investment was drastically increased.

Instead of revising the agricultural policy and carrying out reforms in the management of industry, with the overall aim of removing the imbalance in the economy and better utilising existing resources, Gierek could be accused of accelerating industrial growth while retaining the economic system and pursuing a policy which could not possibly sustain that growth, that is, of preparing the stage for an economic catastrophe.

Many investment projects were completed, thanks to loans and foreign imports, in record time, but at the same time the Western debt grew from 0 in 1970 to 2.5 billion dollars in 1973 and 11 billion in 1975 (Mieszczankowski, 1980). In January 1976 the cost of servicing it reached 27.7 per cent of the value of the yearly exports of goods and services. Since the acceptable safe limit is assumed to be no more than 25 per cent and the volume of debt kept on increasing, uneasiness about the economic situation was growing as was made explicit in the official report of the experts (*Nowe Drogi*, 10-11, 1980, p.239).

It became obvious that the economy was unable to sustain a further growth of debt. The first step the authorities contemplated in order to break this vicious circle was to cut imports of meat, grain and fodder, and even to use Polish agricultural produce for export. This would necessitate a considerable rise in food prices to maintain the balance of the food market, and this the authorities decided to do in June 1976. However, as in 1970, this decision was met by a wave of protests and riots which compelled the government to abandon its plans. An economic decline set in, which could not be offset at the cost of the consumer; this accounted for the increase in the share of consumption in the national income from 66 per cent in 1975 to 74 per cent in 1979 which in turn happened at the expense of investments.

The spending cuts affected all industries and had a devastating effect on the volume of exports. The burden of foreign debt not only weighed heavily on the economy, but increased from one year to another. Many industries were not able to use their full capacity because of the drastic reduction of imports from hard-currency countries of raw materials and other goods indispensable to production. Cheap food meant that expenditure on food subsidies was rising from one year to another; attempts to activate agriculture necessitated supplies of fodder, fertilisers and equipment from abroad; and since the agricultural output expected as a result of these imports did not materialise in sufficient quantities in due time, food had to be imported on a massive scale, increasing the volume of debt. The volume of exports and its direction in the years 1976–9 also compared unfavourably with previous years (see Główczyk, 1981).

The recession in the West and the rising price of oil contributed to Poland's negative balance of trade with the capitalist countries, but Polish export to socialist countries was also reduced which suggests that the causes of the crisis were not due to the recession only.

The reduction of national income was inevitable in conditions of decreasing imports and the increasing burden of debt-servicing. Table 3·4 illustrates this trend.

Table 3·4 The annual rate of growth of national income (in fixed prices) in percentages

	Output produced	Output for domestic use
1966–70	6.0	5.8
1971–75	9.8	12.0
1976–79	3.1	1.7

Source: Rydygier (1980)

This table illustrates the collapse of the economic strategy adopted in 1970, and reveals the dilemma faced by Gierek's government. The critics of Gierek in the party élites try to argue that an alternative economic policy did exist and blame the failure of the policies in the seventies on the mistakes and voluntarism of the party bosses, drunk with the successes of the first two years and oblivious to the arguments and objections of the experts. Such explanations, however, only play down the nature of the system and political circumstances after December 1970. Gierek and his team tried to operate in the face of social tensions and pressures they were unable to overcome; and within a command economy system, the rules of which they had to follow. The tasks undertaken by the leadership which assumed power in the wake of the events of 1970–1 were tantamount to trying to square the circle within the framework of bureaucratic economic management. We would suggest that to focus criticism on the ruling clique of the nineteen-seventies, its policies, incompetence and low moral standards is in fact an effort to screen from criticism 'the real socialism', that is, the command economy and authoritarian rule.

The point can be illustrated by a more detailed analysis of some of the most sensitive areas of the economy where the nature of the system manifested itself very clearly: investments, agricultural development and price and income policy. In all these areas errors of judgement and misguided decisions were certainly contributing factors to the subsequent economic catastrophe, but the main problem consisted in the imbalances of the economic processes bureaucratic management was supposed to control.

THE IMBALANCES IN INVESTMENT PLANNING

Well-planned investments are crucial to the success of economic policy but, as we have said before, in all Communist command economies investment activities have the inherent tendency to create imbalances which affect the objectives set up by the planning authorities. Delays in completion of investment projects, investment in low-priority areas, neglect of investments vital for balanced development of the economy, preference for traditional industries at the expense of the most advanced ones, are endemic diseases of centralised decision making (see Józefiak, 1980).

The two related questions, how much investment and what kind, were always crucial for Communist economies, but their importance increased even more at a time of accelerated growth when the potential impact of under-utilisation of massive resources was intensified. A few years later, that is at the beginning of the nineteen-eighties, when this growth was brought to an abrupt halt and the imbalances of the economic structure became evident, the following aspects of misguided investment policy were highlighted:

1) The neglect of many industries of vital importance which had become the bottlenecks of the economy. The green light was given, for instance, for the expansion of the electrical and mechanical engineering industry at the expense of the fuel and power industry, without which economic development could not proceed.

Transport was another neglected area which was soon to pose most serious problems for running the economy. Difficulties in transporting raw materials and agricultural products created insurmountable problems in the later seventies when there were no means for any substantial improvements.

Investments aiming at the protection of the environment have also been severely neglected creating enormous problems especially in providing adequate water supplies and curbing damage to agriculture and health in industrial areas.

Another characteristic of unbalanced investment policy was the neglect of vital industries supplying both the producer and consumer with manufactured products of vital importance—the timber and paper industries, light industry and the food industry—a neglect which accounted for the subsequent shortages of basic commodities.

The net results of investment policy found their reflection in the changes of structure of Polish industry which reveal deep disproportions between different sectors of the economy (see Szefler, 1983).

2) The second destabilising tendency in the nineteen-seventies was the preference for investment in large-scale enterprises at the expense of existing small firms and workshops which for many years had supplied the needs of many important areas of the economy. So-called local industry was practically wiped out at a stroke with the exception of one or two areas (see Rakowski, 1981a). The effects of this policy were particularly devastating in the pharmaceutical industry where small firms produced vital products. Large-scale technology became dominant also in the building industry which had previously consisted of many local enterprises. This caused an enormous increase in

costs due to the investment in house-factories and to the huge consumption of power by the cement works on which the new technology relied.

There was also a general tendency to give priority to the building of new enterprises at the expense of improving and modernising existing ones.

3) Another feature of investment policy was the tendency to direct funds towards highly urbanised areas, where the impact of investment on the environment was particularly detrimental, and the shortages of labour and public amenities most acute. In addition, many investments in less developed regions of the country consisted mainly of office buildings or sumptuous recreational centres at the expense of hospitals, health service centres, public transport facilities and sanitary installations.

4) Finally, there was too much investment undertaken at once in conditions of limited material and human resources, which resulted in the inevitable dragging on of construction of new plants, the freezing of many investments for which the resources were lacking and enormous losses due to frozen assets and lack of expected output which had already been included in plans for further investment projects (see also Lewycky, 1981, on the role of joint ventures in Comecon).

Table 3·5 Structure of investments

	State of implementation (in milliards zloty)			
	1975	1979	1980	1st quarter 1981
Frozen investments	306.7	664.8	779.9	802.3
Average cycle of implementation in months	30.3	38.6	38.8	
Productivity of durable resources in zloty per 1,000 zloty of gross value of fixed capital	407	324	287	

Source: *Więcej prawdy o inwestycjach, Z materiałów GUSu*, str.2, 1981, p.2.

The rate of accumulation was staggering. The share of accumulation in national income for the years 1970–8 was as follows:

Table 3·6 Accumulation as percentage of national income, 1970–8

1970	27.0
1971	29.3
1972	31.6
1973	35.2
1974	38.0
1975	35.5
1976	34.5
1978	30.8

Source: Bombera (1980)

The original plans for 1971–5 assumed a limited growth with investments amounting to 21.3 per cent of the national income which made rapid improvement in living standards rather unlikely (see Mieszczankowski, 1980), but already by the end of 1972 a new direction was adopted: it was assumed that the rate of accumulation would grow without impairing living standards and that real incomes would rapidly improve owing to the growth of labour productivity. According to Mieszczankowski (1980) the real rate of accumulation was even higher than indicated in official statistics, because of the lower prices of investment goods, and was one of the highest in the world.

This brief summary, which is by no means complete, illustrates the imbalances of so-called centralised planning in the command economy of Poland in the nineteen-seventies. All these deficiencies appeared under Gomułka's rule as well but were kept within certain limits because of his cautious economic policy. Moreover, in a situation where foreign loans played only a minor part in economic development, danger signals in the form of raw-material shortages or inadequate supplies of equipment for newly-constructed factories appeared much earlier and compelled the authorities to carry out the necessary measures including curbing the investment drive.

The snowball effect was felt very early: borrowing created a new spiral of self-reinforcing tendencies:

1) Increased imports from abroad made it necessary to cover the deficit by foreign credits.
2) The growing volume of debts necessitated the growth of industries producing for exports, i.e., encouraged further loans for investment and modernisation of the economy.
3) Modernisation implied the acquisition of foreign licences, i.e., extended the necessity for foreign loans.
4) Foreign licences and modernised industries made the country more and more dependent on foreign supplies of certain raw materials, semi-finished products and spare parts, which increased the trade deficit even further.
5) The accelerated rate of industrial growth encouraged factories to buy abroad even those components which could have been produced in Poland.
6) The need to repay the loans and service them, in conditions of a high trade deficit, meant taking further loans on less favourable terms, i.e. aggravated Poland's position from one year to another.
7) The recession in the West operated in the same direction because Polish export was facing ever tougher competition in foreign markets.

The limited decentralisation of the Polish economy contributed to irresponsible borrowing from abroad and discouraged the development of subsidiary production at home.

Enterprises were able to obtain from the state foreign-currency allocations without any costs involved. This situation created a rush to import equipment and products and materials which with some minor investments could have been obtainable on the home market. Foreign imports were, moreover, unrelated to profits gained by the respective enterprises in foreign markets; in many cases the cost of imported components alone was higher than the value of the final products sold at home or the export market prices.

THE INDIVIDUAL FARMER AND THE COMMAND ECONOMY

All economists seem to agree that cheap food and high

prices for industrial products, including agricultural equipment and fuel, are virtually incompatible in advanced Communist economies, unless compulsory deliveries of farm produce are enforced or foodstuffs are heavily subsidised. In the first case, incentives for increased production in agriculture are weakened or eliminated. In the second case there is an excessive demand for agricultural products, recycling of some food products for agricultural needs (feeding cattle with excess bread sold in state shops is an example) and permanent shortages in the shops.

In Poland the above-mentioned dilemma compelled Gomułka to raise the price of meat in 1964 and 1970. Faced by a firm stand of the workers on the issue of food prices in 1970–1, Gierek tried at first to reconcile the interests of the peasants and of the urban population by maintaining subsidised prices and removing the pressure of compulsory deliveries.

In the first few years the new policy coincided with excellent harvests. Agricultural production increased rapidly. Many peasants who found employment in industry were able to invest their incomes in farming by buying new equipment and machinery. The free market encouraged the development of fruit and vegetable growing, and high prices paid for livestock and poultry resulted in a rapid increase in the number of broilers, pigs and cattle on individual farms.

The pledge to freeze food prices for the consumer did not stimulate, however, sound long-term development. Cheap food, heavy subsidies, resources directed primarily to the production of industrial goods undermined the balance between agriculture and industry and led to the classic dilemma of the 'open scissors' so characteristic of all earlier attempts at accelerated industrialisation.

Increased wages brought about a much increased demand for agricultural products. To the extent that demand was met the cost of food subsidies shot up. While in 1970 the subsidies paid by the state to farmers amounted to 7.5 billion zloty—in 1980 they reached the sum of 170 billion zloty (Wrzaszczyk, 1980, p.108).

At the same time, imports of grain and fodder became a necessity so as to provide the population with bread and other basic foods and to help the farmers to maintain and develop their livestock and poultry production. It was argued that it was cheaper to provide farmers with fodder, including grain, purchased by the state for hard currency than to buy more meat in Western countries. What has not been publicly acknowledged was the inability of the government to curb the demand for meat and meat products in a situation of stable food prices and rising incomes. The determination to allow the country to live beyond its means for a prolonged time was due to the political situation and it was this policy which caused the final disaster.

The income of individual peasants lagged visibly behind those of state employees:

Table 3·7 Individual peasants' income as a percentage of state employees' earnings

	Nominal earnings	Real earnings
1970	72.9	77.1
1971	79.8	79.8
1972	84.0	82.5
1973	81.9	80.1
1974	76.1	74.1
1975	70.3	68.1
1976	78.1	71.7
1977	82.4	73.7

Source: Banaszkiewicz (1980)

If in 1974 the production of livestock stagnated, in 1975 it fell by 2.1 per cent and in 1976 by a further 1.1 per cent. The number of pigs fell from 21.5 million in 1974 to 21.3 million in 1975, 18.8 million in 1977 and 16.7 million in January 1979. (Bojko, 1980). Wherein lay the causes of this decline of livestock? It was neither intended nor welcomed by the leadership which was committed to rapid improvement of the living standards of the population. The explanation is to be sought not only in the strategy of accelerated growth but in the clash between the command economy and the interests of individual peasants.

1) There was a process of depopulation of the countryside, which provided the labour force for industry. Well-paid

jobs in industry meant that the villages emptied of young people, and the increase in the average age of the labour force in agriculture proceeded inexorably. In the years 1970–5, employment in private farms fell by 1,451,000 while according to plans it was to be increased by 300,000.

2) Increased pressure on finances and resources for industrial growth reduced the volume of raw materials, machinery and products required for the modernisation of farms: in the whole decade not a single fertiliser factory was built, production of tractors did not increase, and supplies of basic tools diminished from one year to the next.

3) Cheap food prices operated as a disincentive: individual peasants found it cheaper to buy food than to produce it, especially in view of the increased prices of the goods they needed for food production. At the same time, there were more and more incentives to produce industrial crops at the expense of animal and grain production.

4) The depopulation of individual farms resulted in land being sold off to urban dwellers for summer houses or to the state in exchange for pension rights. Much of the land acquired by the state farms or the State Fund (Państwowy Fundusz Ziemi) was neglected by the new owners or simply left unattended.

All this compelled the government to take counter measures. In the long run, they saw the solution in enlarging the state sector in agriculture, where they believed modernisation could be implemented in a more effective way, and links between agricultural production and state-owned industry could be reinforced. In the short term, however, special inducements and extraordinary measures were directed at each peasant. Pressures were exercised in 1975–6 to compel peasants to sell grain to the state. If they did not comply, local authorities used all kinds of sanctions. For instance, they refused to issue any official papers, which some of the recalcitrant peasants might have needed, imposed fees in grain for marriages, ordered schoolchildren to supply a levy of several kilograms of grain from the farms, etc.

The sale of land to peasants was temporarily halted: while in 1971–3 individual peasants bought 73 per cent of the land sold by the State Land Fund, in 1974 their share fell to 20 per cent and in 1975 to 5 per cent.

At the same time, the policy of vigorously encouraging the development of state farms and co-operatives was pursued. The State Land Fund gradually became the main instrument for the acquisition of land for state farms, and other collective agricultural establishments.

At first sight it seemed that the state farms offered a real chance of boosting agricultural productivity. In some provinces of northern Poland the economic weight of the state farms was indeed enormous. In the province of Koszalin they occupied 73 per cent of the area; Gorzów—67.4 per cent; Elbleg—62.4 per cent; Olsztyn—61 per cent and Jelenia Góra—61 per cent (most of these are in ex-German territory) (Świderski, 1981).

Apparently Gierek genuinely believed that high-level technology applied in state farms and collective farms, would solve agricultural problems 'at a stroke'. The development of 'food factories' was an important part of this strategy.

The slogan of developing socialist agriculture became the guideline of government policy. Whatever was available for the needs of agriculture was directed towards 'socialist' farms. Their deficit was covered by state subsidies. Forcible purchase of land from individual peasants increased rapidly.

All these measures did not prevent the deepening of the food crisis—on the contrary, they aggravated it (see Brus, 1983b).

1) The imbalance between the funds allocated for the development of individual farms and state and collective farms increased. In 1978 the direct subsidy per 1 ha was 10,222 zloty for state farms and 19,000 zloty for collective farms, compared with 777 zloty for individual peasants (Kwiatkowski and Żukowski, 1981).

2) The effects of this expenditure were disappointing: while the net production of individual farmers grew in the years 1970-9 by 13.9 billion zloty and their invested capital by 179 billion, the socialised sector increased its invested capital by 155 billion zloty, but its net production in 1979 was 4.8 billion zloty less than in 1970.

3) Material supplies directed to individual peasants were also substantially reduced; especially as far as fertilisers were concerned, the amount allocated to individual peasants was half of that allocated to state and co-operative farms. Deliveries of equipment and spare parts for individual farms, always in short supply, were further reduced and coal was often unobtainable.

4) The public sector proved unable to utilise in full the opportunities offered by the state. Wastage and theft reached unbelievable proportions. Many technologies proved inadequate and the much advertised mass-breeding of cattle proved to be a total disaster.

The animal factories (which, as mentioned above, proved to be a typical example of the misfortunes of accelerated modernisation) were built on foreign licences with little regard to the realities of climate, organisation of production and marketing, qualifications of the labour force and availability of fodder and equipment. They also increased dependence on imported fodder and materials. The output proved in many cases out of proportion to the costs involved.

5) The discouragement of the private sector resulted in further migration from the country to the towns. In one village regarded as typical in a journalist's report, 70 per cent of the farmers were over 50, 20 per cent between 30 and 50, and 10 per cent below 30 (Wołosiuk, 1981). According to Błażynski (1979, p.184) by 1976 nearly half of the population in the villages was over 70 years old.

It should be noted that for many years high yields were achieved in farms owned by individuals employed in state industry ('worker-peasants'). They were able to use their earnings, and often industrial 'know-how' to improve their farms. According to an inquiry carried out by the Institute of Agricultural Economics, they supplied about 15 per cent of agricultural produce and 13 per cent of the global produce of individual peasants. Their productivity per hectare was higher than in other individual farms and much higher than in state farms and collective farms. In global figures, the farms run by 'worker-peasants' supplied more than the whole socialist sector (Bogacz, 1980).

The needs of this category of peasants, however, were completely ignored and in the late nineteen-seventies they even became the target of direct discrimination which contributed to a great extent to the deepening food crisis.

Efforts to stimulate the state and co-operative sector of agriculture thus posed more problems than they solved. The state farms required enormous investments which often did not pay. The more resources were redirected towards state farms, the less could be released for individual farmers, who had to cut their investments because of the shortage of machinery and building materials. The policy of increasing state land resources became, in itself, a serious obstacle to further development of agriculture, since many efficient farmers were not able to extend their individual land-holdings. As usual, the shortage of resources for investments was reflected in the development of the 'parallel market', in which the private producer was forced into all sorts of shady deals with suppliers and administrators. This included the bribery of officials, outright purchase of stolen products and other illegal activities.

The best illustration of the failure of the public sector to deliver the goods is the following relationship between the productivity of labour in state and co-operative farms and individual farms:

Table 3·8 Productivity in individual and public sector farms

	Individual farms	State and collective farms
Global production of grains (kilograms per hectare)	950	840
Fodder utilised (kilograms per hectare)	920	1,150
Animal products (kilograms per hectare)	336	284
Fodder utilised per 1 kilogram of animal production (in kilograms)	2.74	4.06
Net value of final production in thousands zloty per hectare	+3.7	−0.5

Source: Grochowski (1980)

Changes in the ownership of arable land in the years 1970–9 are characteristic for the whole agricultural policy in those years.

Table 3·9 Change in the ownership of arable land, 1970–9 (in hectares)

	1970		1979	
	area	*percentage*	*area*	*percentage*
Individual farms	12,636,500	83.7	11,108,500	75.8
State farms	2,198,600	14.6	2,737,500	18.7
Collective farms	193,500	1.3	503,600	3.4
Other state land (including State Land Fund)	61,300	0.4	302,100	2.0
Total	15,089,900	100.0	14,651,700	100.0

Source: Staar (1982), p.178.

Various administrative measures supporting the policy of 'socialisation' of Polish agriculture contributed to the further deterioration of the position of the private farmers. Lipservice was paid to the rights of private peasants to their property, but in fact they were squeezed out by various economic and administrative measures. If in 1970 a farm of five hectares of land yielded an average income equal to that in the public sector, in 1980 a farmer needed ten hectares to get this result (Bojko, 1981). Production of small-scale equipment for private farms was cut down, tools like scythes were often unobtainable, machinery collectively owned by individual peasants was transferred to pseudo-cooperatives and the original owners were discriminated against in the use of this machinery. New laws regulating the transfer of agricultural property were introduced. Practices of harrassment and discrimination against individual peasants were tolerated, quantities of fertilisers and fodder allocated to individual buyers were strictly limited. All this contributed to the creation of an atmosphere of insecurity and resulted in a collapse of the breeding of animals in smaller private farms at a time when the public sector could achieve no more than fill the gap.

As we see, agriculture was subject to a double squeeze. On the one hand it was affected by the impact of accelerated industrialisation which directed national resources towards industry at the expense of the agricultural sector. On the other hand, mounting difficulties led the authorities to favour the public sector at the expense of the private farmer. And since the public sector was much more dependent on imports of fodder and equipment, once foreign credits became difficult to obtain and imports had to be cut, the country faced growing shortages of basic foodstuffs.

A RECIPE FOR HYPERINFLATION

The effects of too much money chasing too few goods vary with the nature of the economy: in a market economy in these circumstances we face rising prices, in a command economy where prices are regulated by the state and for one reason or another kept stable, the shops will be empty, there will be long queues, waiting lists and, if necessary, rationing of consumer goods.

To the extent in which a command economy is accompanied by a parallel private market, prices in the latter will soar according to the law of supply and demand, but even there price movements are distorted by the monopolistic position of many sellers and the scarcity of some consumer goods.

Gierek's dilemma as far as inflation was concerned was pretty simple: he had to respect his commitment to stable prices, while the incomes of the population were rising and massive supplies of consumer goods and foodstuffs were needed to maintain the balance. As mentioned he hoped to close the gap in the short run by stimulating agricultural output and using foreign loans to import consumer goods, and he expected that in the long run accelerated growth would provide the means of repaying the loans.

Thus the authorities decided to maintain a high and rising rate of accumulation and to stimulate industrial growth, *and at the same time* to improve living standards and keep prices low. Even in 1975, when the failure of the new policy was evident, it was officially stated 'it is out of the question to abandon the active policy of increasing individual incomes which began in 1971' (Kisiel, 1975, p.94). This policy was bound, however, to end with hyperinflation. Prices were frozen at a time when the purchasing power of the population was rapidly growing while, in the quest for quick development, many resources were redirected from the consumers' to the producers' market. As the loans utilised to cover the gap were not inexhaustible, the inevitable shortages of consumer goods were on the increase and repressed inflation found its expression in the so-called inflationary overhang, that is, the growing amount of money owned by the population which was not offset by the available market supplies.

An *ad hoc* solution was sought after some time by introducing a system of double prices for meat and meat products: alongside the official prices so-called 'commercial' prices were established and special shops offered products for customers who disliked queueing and were able to pay the higher prices. Disguised price rises also became a common practice: cheaper brands of goods were replaced by more expensive ones without any improvement in quality. The sale of scarce goods for foreign currency was facilitated; citizens were permitted to use their foreign currency in such transactions freely, without having to account for its possession. Foreign currency became a parallel means of exchange which, in conditions of the staggering rate of exchange of foreign currency for zlotys on the black market, contributed to the reinforcement of a dual price system; one based on state decisions, and the other reflecting the market equilibrium.

The nominal monetary income of the population between 1970 and 1975 virtually doubled. In 1975 when the cost of investment went over the 500 billion zloty mark, almost half of it constituted the cost of labour, that is, was due to the increased purchasing power of the population (Kisiel, 1975). At the same time, the role of consumer goods imports started to decrease: while imported goods constituted 6.9 per cent of the volume of the market supplies in 1970 and 9.1 per cent in 1972, in 1974 their share fell to 8 per cent while the pressure on internal resources due to accelerating accumulation was already felt.

The rising prices of many industrial goods became in themselves a factor of low labour productivity in the enterprises and diverted production away from the consumer market. The enterprises could theoretically achieve a higher margin of profitability in the following three ways, or by a combination of them: (a) coming to the market with better and more attractive products; (b) reducing the cost of production by reorganising the labour processes; and (c) increasing arbitrarily the prices of their products. In practice, the enterprises followed the third way as the easiest and most profitable. According to GUS (Central Statistical Office) (Siwoń, 1983), in global industrial production, goods for private consumption constitute in general no more than 20 per cent: *the rest is sold to other producers* (tools, machinery, semi-finished products) and to various agencies of the state (armaments, health and transport equipment, etc.) or remains with the producer as his 'stock'. As one of the commentators pointed out, neither the state nor the enterprises were as sensitive to low quality and high prices as the individual consumers, a situation which not only favoured many price increases, but also encouraged the enterprises to work primarily for the public sector at the expense of the consumer market (Siwoń, 1983). The phenomenon of 'industry working for industry' was thus reinforced while the rising prices of many commodities encouraged further inflationary wage claims.

One way of correcting the imbalance between supply and demand was to increase labour productivity: hence technological change was supported by many economists as an answer to market difficulties. In other words, inflationary pressures were supposed to justify accelerated growth which meant adding momentum to the vicious circle of the Polish economy.

The political effects of excess demand over supply were most alarming. In a command economy the government was naturally blamed for everything: rising prices, shortages, inadequate pay rises, the poor quality of goods. There was a general belief that prices and wages depended on the government. Hence public opinion, including factions within the establishment, was turning against the central leadership which was accused of mismanagement and indifference to the needs of the consumers.

The size of the pay packet was becoming ineffective as an incentive because pay rises were regarded primarily as a compensation for rising prices and shortages of cheaper products. The acquisition of moderately priced commodities demanded great perseverance in queueing, and became a matter of privilege, abuse or sheer luck.

In any other Communist society the answer to this situation was to set prices to match the existing level of supplies and to allow incomes to rise only if the output for the consumer market increased. But, since the first attempt by Gierek to regulate prices in 1976 failed, each successive year contributed to the further growth of both hidden and open inflation.

The situation was becoming so alarming that even the opposition embodied in KOR (The Workers' Defence Committee) regarded the reform of prices to be an inevitable means of restoring some balance to the economy. In an analysis published by KOR with an introduction by Professor Edward Lipiński, we read:

Among the immediate steps to be taken, the most important we think is a return to economic equilibrium. This would necessitate adjustments in respect not only to supply, that is, production will have to be increased, but also to demand which would mean only a moderate increase in people's incomes as well as of prices. We also think that it is essential initially to decrease the people's total purchasing power somewhat, that is, increase prices without providing a simultaneous supplementary compensation. (KOR 1978, p.20)

In all aspects of the economic policies we have so far discussed, the competition for national resources between different lobbies and decisions enforced by them contributed to the increase of economic imbalance associated with accelerated growth. This would be regarded as normal and, to an extent, manageable in an autocratically operated command economy. Decisions about allocation of resources for investments to different sections of industry, and about the share in public funds allocated to agriculture, to services, to the development of the infrastructure, all are part of a complicated power game in Communist economies. But under Gierek a new powerful factor in this interplay appeared: it consisted of the 'consumer lobby' represented by the workers who resisted any modification of prices and incomes policy. The economy was thus disrupted by a new set-up in power relationships incompatible with the requirements of the command economy.

If we regard the ensuing economic and political crises as a price which must be paid for accelerated modernisation within this new framework, the question must be answered as to what was achieved during the decade of the nineteen-seventies. Indeed, the effects of the first four to five years of Gierek's leadership were outstanding, but if measure is taken of the whole decade, the overall results were not much higher than those achieved in the nineteen-sixties. Mikołajczyk, a Polish economist, summarised (1980) these effects as follows:

a) The average rate of national income growth was 6 per cent in the nineteen-sixties, and 6.8 per cent in the nineteen-seventies, but the drop in 1980 obliterated even this difference.

b) The dynamics of industrial growth were roughly the same; there was only the difference in the annual growth in B-industries by 2 per cent in the seventies [offset by the collapse of manufacturing production in the early eighties—M.H.].

c) The dynamics of agriculture were again roughly the same; there was an enormous rate of growth of animal farms, but hardly any growth in animal breeding in the economy as a whole.

d) Investments in absolute terms were higher in 1971 and so was productive potential, but shortages of labour became a bottleneck.

If, on top of that, the human cost of shortages in the Polish economy after 1980 and the huge debt that remains to be paid are taken into account, the record of Gierek's decade is hardly encouraging. It justified in full Gomułka's ridicule of 'socialism in a tail coat' as different from his alleged 'socialism in a peasant's tunic'.

As far as comparisons with the economic development of other East European countries are concerned, the failure of Gierek to achieve what other Communist regimes in Eastern Europe have achieved, while pursuing the same objectives and exposed to similar mistakes, is most spectacular. As we have said before, all East European countries opted for dash for growth and consumerism in their economic policies. The problems they faced were also strikingly similar: they all relied too much on foreign loans and over-estimated their own ability to repay them. They were affected by multiple rises of oil prices and inflationary pressures. Many of them were compelled at a certain stage to carry out substantial price increases to balance the consumer market (Portes, 1980).

However, there was a fundamental difference between Poland and other Communist countries (see Hare and Wanless, 1981). Poland was the only country in which the authorities had to yield to the demands of the masses resisting the deterioration of their living standards. As we have mentioned before, the mass movements in 1970 and 1976 made their mark on the whole economic policy implemented in the seventies in Poland. The power of the masses was, however, purely negative. The workers were able to prevent an economic policy which aimed at the restoration of economic balance at the expense of their living standards but they were not strong enough to enforce the transformation of the rules according to which the economy and society in a Communist country are being run. The result was a development which was bound to end with a staggering economic collapse.

4 Economic stratification in a crisis-ridden society

Official Communist doctrine does not deny the existence of inequality in Eastern Europe. It justifies the economic differences between different groups by the functional requirements of the system. This is covered by the Marxist formula from the *Critic of the Gotha Programme*: people have to participate in the national income in proportion to their contribution in producing it. In Lenin's words this meant: from each according to his ability, to each according to his work, and, as one Polish author recently declared

The model of a developed socialist society has two in-built principles which never occurred together in pre-socialist types of societies. These are the principles of economic effectiveness and dynamism and the principle of social justice. Until socialism emerged as a social and economic system, economic effectiveness and dynamism were being achieved with complete disregard for justice. Economy and morality, social reality and humanistic ideas were—if not aloud, then silently treated as contradictory elements. (Wesołowski, 1980, p.35)

This declaration which might be perfectly justified as reflecting socialist ideals is, however, a far cry from the realities of societies where economic differences by no means depend exclusively on the requirements of economic effectiveness and dynamism. The above quotation is thus a statement expressing the basic myth of the official ideology; it refers to society not as it is but as it ought to be, while pretending that it reflects real facts of life.

A second widespread myth is that of the exclusive role of earnings in personal incomes, as opposed to social parasitism, the acquisition of wealth by exploitation, through interplay of market forces, etc. Even a distinguished Western economist once declared: 'For practical purposes, it may be assumed that under socialism income, if we exclude social service benefits, is derived from one's own labour . . . Exceptions to this rule are of minor consequence . . . .' (Wilczyński, 1972, p.118).

86

A series of studies published in the nineteen-sixties, seventies and beginning of the eighties, for example, studies by Djilas (1966). Matthews (1978), Nove (1975), or Smolar (1983) considerably modified this view.

They show that in Communist countries income is not derived from work only, and income differentials are subject to principles unrelated to work performance; they very often depend on the position on the ladder of privileges associated with the positions on the ladder of administrative hierarchies. The theory of the new class elaborated in the above-mentioned studies emphasises thus the parasitic character of income distribution with regard to the party–state bureaucracy.

The differentiation of incomes is, however, far more complicated than that, particularly in conditions of the mixed economy in which market forces play a considerable part in reinforcing economic inequality. The latter issue has been elaborated in many studies dealing with the so-called 'secondary, parallel, unregistered or black economy' (although the last concept is rather misleading, because in all Communist societies the role of the private sector is formally recognised).

Istvén Kemány enumerates the following features of the unregistered and unplanned economy in Hungary (the same applies to other Communist countries as well although to varying degrees):

1) The legalised private sector and its market transactions, both legal and illegal.
2) Transactions within the legally unrecognised private sector.
3) Supplementary earnings received for illicit dealings in regular work, i.e. 'inbuilt' earnings but socially uncondoned.
4) Gratuities for work performed within the scope of regular employment but outside the bounds of professional duty.
5) Transactions by directors for the purposes of obtaining and retaining manpower.
6) Market transactions by the managerial staff for the purposes of ensuring the material conditions of production.

7) Informal transactions between workers to ensure the material conditions of production.
8) Market ventures by directors of enterprises.
9) Payments made to persons who misuse their power in order to render services, i.e. bribery (Kemány, 1982).

Many of these activities affect, in one way or another, the living standards of people involved in them but, except for incomes of peasants, tradesmen and craftsmen (i.e. officially registered individuals operating as entrepreneurs), are not reflected by official statistics.

Inequality in Communist societies, whatever its origin, has been increasing with the advancement of the policies of consumerism, that is, in the nineteen-sixties and early nineteen-seventies, but its effect on the attitudes of the public was to some extent attenuated by the fact that, on balance, most people felt better off and expected a further improvement of their living standards.

The situation changed in the late nineteen-seventies and early nineteen-eighties when in most East European countries further rises of real wages became exceedingly difficult. The question arose of where the cuts should be made and restraints imposed. Moreover, in view of the uncontrollable forces affecting the distribution and redistribution of the national wealth, it was not at all clear to what extent the state was able to pursue a policy of social justice.

The changing indices of nominal and real wage increases and prices in the early and late nineteen-seventies point to the new difficulties experienced by many East European countries in satisfying expectations of a continuous improvement of living standards.

As we see from the table 4·1, almost all East European countries experienced an increase of real wages in the early seventies and a decline in the late seventies. As we shall see, Poland was, for many reasons, much more affected by these trends than other Communist countries. It should also be emphasised that the official data fail to reflect reality in at least two important points: (1) The official figures of real wage changes do not reflect the full impact of concealed inflation (and partly also open inflation in secondary market commodities) on the living standards. (2) The average positive and negative growth of overall real wages does not give any clue as to the impact of these changes on different social groups.

Table 4·1 Indices of nominal and real wages and of prices (average annual increases in percentages)

Country		1971-75	1976-80
Czechoslovakia	nominal wages	3.5	2.8
	cost of living	0.1	2.1
	real wages	3.5	0.7
GDR	nominal wages	4.8	3.0
	cost of living	−0.3	0.1
	real wages	5.3	4.4
Hungary	nominal wages	6.2	7.0
	cost of living	2.8	6.3
	real wages	3.3	0.7
Rumania	nominal wages	4.4	7.0
	cost of living	0.5	1.4
	real wages	3.7	5.2
Bulgaria	nominal wages	3.4	4.5
	cost of living	0.5	3.9
	real wages	2.9	0.6
USSR	nominal wages	3.7	3.0
	cost of living	0.0	0.6
	real wages	4.4	3.4
Poland	nominal wages	9.8	8.8
	cost of living	2.4	6.8
	real wages	7.2	1.9

Source: Bauer (1983), p.282.

A full assessment of the influence of economic change in the seventies on economic stratification in Poland requires a more detailed analysis of the various sources of income and the evaluation of their dynamics in view of the inflationary trends of the late seventies.

EGALITARIANISM AND ECONOMIC SCARCITY

In all Communist countries early industrialisation was associated with a drastic reduction in living standards.

Unlike the early reconstruction period (1945–8), the first post-war industrialisation plans in Eastern Europe in 1949–55 brought deprivation, undernourishment and squalor. In Poland economic scarcity coexisted with economic and social inequality, which was, however, mitigated by the limited resources which were at the government's disposal. Although the privileges of party and state officials were openly acknowledged, the overall low standard of living was in itself a major factor limiting the scope of administrative privileges. Access to a canteen serving decent three-course lunches, a modest two-bedroom flat, the use of a chauffeur-driven car or the chance to buy imported fruit and garments of the kind sold in the West in cheap department stores, were at that time regarded as luxuries associated with high offices.

The effort to keep the economy in balance contributed to the low level of consumption. The equilibrium between inadequate supply and demand was maintained by means of drastic price increases, wage restraint and, when necessary, by change of currency which reduced hoarded money and savings to a fraction of their former value. Such monetary reforms were, at some time or another, carried out in all Communist countries (in Poland, monetary reform came in 1950). In spite of such drastic measures the gap between the amount of money paid to state employees and the scarce supplies of goods persisted, and made it necessary to resort in Poland to meat rationing and, in January 1953, a general increase in prices was introduced. Retail prices grew by about 50 per cent, and this was only partly compensated by modest pay rises, and increases in some social benefits.

Similar steps were taken in other East European countries. With a few exceptions, hardly any group in Eastern Europe escaped the fall in living standards caused by these policies, though the privileged were more cushioned from it than the rest of the population. It is no wonder that after Stalin's death opposition to these policies was growing and the desire for improvement in living standards was forcefully expressed.

The new policy of redressing the balance in favour of the consumer market contributed to the gradual improvement of living standards in Eastern Europe and widened the stratum of people whose economic position was better than the average. The trend was reinforced in some countries where, in a kind of a trade-off of consumerism against depoliticisation, the efforts of the government were directed towards a rapid expansion of the consumer market.

Unlike the early post-war period, when scarce 'extras' were unobtainable except by direct allocation by the state, incomes, i.e. money, started to play an ever-growing part in obtaining many coveted commodities: good food, television sets, cars and even flats became gradually accessible to those in the higher income brackets. At the same time, the effort to revitalise the economy brought in many countries a new life to private production and commerce and the impact of market forces on the redistribution of many economic benefits grew accordingly, increasing social inequalities.

It is interesting that in post-1956 Poland, where the liberalisation of the regime went further than elsewhere, the trade-off between consumerism and depoliticisation was much less evident: the new policy pursued by Gomułka allowed for only a moderate increase in consumption. Moreover, members of the party and state bureaucracy who enjoyed a wave of increased prosperity in other Communist countries, suffered a serious setback in Poland in 1956: in the days preceding Gomułka's return to power, their privileges were publicly denounced and many 'perks' were banned, including the so-called 'shops behind yellow curtains' which sold scarce goods to the party and state élites.

Gomułka himself displayed a somewhat puritanical attitude to life. He showed no sympathy with the idea of promoting the sale of more sophisticated goods in the consumer market. He denounced the conspicuous consumption of his subordinates, and emphasised his personal indifference to the small luxuries provided for him.

The perks he did offer to his bureaucrats were rather modest. He was particularly determined to eliminate any sign of corruption among the party and state bureaucracies, and went so far as to insist on the death penalty for people who were found guilty of serious economic crimes even before he managed to introduce legislation to this effect.

He was most anxious to maintain a balanced economy even at the expense of living standards. From time to time, prices were increased rapidly to remove excess money from the market. The price of industrial goods far exceeded the costs of production, and it was standard practice to restrict the salaries of state employees and cut the expenses of the administrative apparatus. In those years, there was a general feeling amongst state officials and the intelligentsia in Poland, that they suffered a lower standard of living than their counterparts in the USSR, Czechoslovakia, Hungary and the German Democratic Republic. On the whole, under Gomułka, the improvement in mass consumption was confined to basic essentials. This policy was characterised by strong egalitarian tendencies which were reflected mainly in the levelling-off of differentials between skilled and semi-skilled workers, and the majority of the so-called working intelligentsia. In these circumstances, the concept of the new class and its economic privileges found less support in Poland than elsewhere. In 1970 Professor Jan Szczepański, referring to 'some well publicised theories of a "new class" composed of the higher ranks of the political apparatus who, profiting from the concentration of political power in their hands, have also secured for themselves economic privileges and the highest income' argued as follows:

This is not true in Poland. The personnel in the political apparatus do not have any special economic privileges, and they are a group on a par with professionals and other categories. Perhaps the asceticism of the first secretary of the Central Committee set a model for the way of life of the political apparatus, for this category actually gets lower salaries than do some other highly specialised categories and make far less than the private entrepreneurs. (Szczepański, 1970, p.123)

Throughout most of the nineteen-sixties, Gomułka's attitude to consumerism was often contrasted with that of Gierek, who was by that time the First Secretary of the Katowice province. Gierek was known to display a genuine interest in improving the level of consumption of key sections of the working population, especially the miners, at the same time doing all he could to improve the living standards of party and state officials in his region. These officials enjoyed many privileges unknown in other parts of Poland: luxurious flats which circumvented the restrictive building regulations, a considerable share in social expenditure, including special rest homes in health resorts, extensive sports facilities, etc.

THE NEW INCOMES POLICY

In 1970 when Gierek came to office as the First Secretary of the Central Committee of the Polish United Workers' Party, his commitment to a policy of high consumption hardly changed. He promised all Poles a better life than they had ever known before.

Low prices, massive imports of foreign consumer products and the erection of sumptuous public buildings, new shops, hotels, and restaurants throughout the whole country marked the new era of consumerism. The prospects for individual prosperity grew considerably, new jobs abounded, generous material incentives were offered, and promotions were readily obtained.

In the early stage of the new policy, it was intended that income differentials should increase to some extent in order to stimulate high productivity. Higher productivity would then, in turn, allow the incomes of the lower paid to be increased at a later stage. The original targets for the differentials between maximum and minimum earnings in the years 1975–90 were designed as follows (Pohorille, 1978):

1975	12.4:1
1980	11.1:1
1985	9.6:1
1990	8.7:1

Yet, with the deterioration in the economic situation, the opposite trend unfolded. The rich became richer than ever before. This development was contrary to the experience of 1949–55 and 1964–70, when economic difficulties affected living standards. The explanation lies partly in the character of the incomes policy adopted by the government and partly in the uncontrolled mechanisms of the economy which will be discussed below.

The policy of operating pay differentials in favour of the bureaucratic élite and technological intelligentsia was regarded by Gierek as a key feature of his new economy. He was deeply convinced that people in leading positions had to be better paid than others, to induce them to carry out their functions in the most effective way.

The advocates of the new policy emphasised the importance of economic incentives of the administrative and managerial apparatus, also as a symbol of their higher status in society. The phrase 'professional career' was restored to the official political vocabulary, and party leaders competed in lavishing favours and benefits on people whose contributions they regarded as essential to the national economy.

The salaries of people occupying top positions in the party–state hierarchy were regulated by the decree of 5 October 1972. The register of incomes included five groups altogether. The highest ones were: Group A, the Chairman of the Council of State and the Prime Minister; Group B, the Chairman of the Parliament, Deputy Prime Ministers, etc.

The salaries consisted of basic pay and a so-called functional allowance which was not regulated by the decree. Those who held the highest offices of state, and lost their posts, were allowed to keep their salary for two years.

The decree stated that its principles should also apply to the leading office-holders in political and social organisations. The provisions made in the decree, concerning the pension rights of leading figures in state, political and social organisations, were more than generous. The people covered by the decree could keep the flats they occupied while in office and were entitled to a 50 per cent reduction in railway fares. The First Secretary of the PUW PCC, the Chairman of the Council of State and the Prime Minister were entitled to 95 per cent of their salary and 'functional allowance' after retirement. Others were offered pensions depending on their age and the number of years of their employment.

The list of privileged officials, apart from the three mentioned above, included the Marshal (speaker) and

Vice-Marshal of Parliament, the deputy chairmen of the State Council, the members and alternate members of the Politbureau, the secretaries and deputy secretaries of the Party Central Committee, the heads of the departments of the Central Committee, the provincial party secretaries, the Chairman of the Supreme Chamber of Control, the President of the Polish Academy of Sciences, ministers and deputy ministers, general directors of the ministries, etc.

Financial privileges were not confined, however, to the highest officials, but were a conspicuous case of a widespread practice of awarding special benefits to selected occupational groups directly linked with the party–state.

Members of the party apparatus, functionaries of the political police, militia men, managerial élites, etc., were awarded special exemptions, rewards and benefits often including a lower retirement age, higher pensions, and the right to claim special benefits in the case of poor health.

According to official figures the monthly salaries of the highest party and state officials in 1981 compared with average monthly wages and salaries were as follows:

Table 4·2 Selected monthly salaries in 1981

Position	Monthly salary in zloty
Premier	28,000
Deputy Premier	25,000
Minister	23,000
Secretary of the Provincial Party Committee	19,000
Head of Department of the Provincial Party Committee in Cracow	11,000
Director of a factory	15,000
Foreman	11,000
Coach driver	7,000

Source: Życie Warszawy, 18 March 1981.

Average salaries and wages were rapidly rising in the first half of the decade in question: for instance, the yearly increase in average pay amounted to 5.3 per cent in 1971 and 14.3 per cent in 1974 (Kabaj, 1980, p.130), but in the years which followed there was no corresponding reduction of the gap between the low and highly paid employees. According to Anna Kuszko, the disparities in pay reached 15:1 in 1978 (Kuszko, 1978). Jan Malanowski (1981) assessed that disparities deduced from official statistics were in fact 22:1 in 1977, but expressed the opinion that real differences were even higher. Significantly, disparities between the average and minimum pay were also increasing.

UNPLANNED PAY DIFFERENTIALS AS A SIDE EFFECT OF ECONOMIC GROWTH

In a discussion of the pay differentials which took place in Poland it has been pointed out that from the very beginning of post-war history all successive governments tried to reduce the differentials between the various economic sectors and occupational groups and every time these attempts failed because of the double-pronged pay policy pursued in the public sector (Kuszko, 1978).

One line consisted in regulating the rates of remuneration so as to leave only differences based on criteria of justice and efficiency: all sorts of special pay scales (tarificators) and guidelines were invented to achieve these objectives. On the other hand, there has always been a tendency to establish efficiency norms which could be surpassed even by 100 and 200 per cent, allocate higher remunerative levels to people lacking the required qualifications, overstep the permitted limits for overtime pay, overlook the breaks in work, offer money for jobs which should have been carried out during a normal working day, etc. (Kuszko, 1978). It should be added that industries which happened to supply products regarded as most important for the national economy also invariably enjoyed considerable advantages not only in terms of the wages and salaries of their employees, but also in their access to extra funds and special bonuses which were intended to motivate people to increased productivity.

Difficulties in maintaining financial discipline, and keeping pay increases and the national pay fund within planned and prescribed limits are experienced by all Communist countries. In conditions of accelerated industrialisation, inflationary pay rises are often necessary in order to recruit and motivate the labour force in those sectors of the economy which are most important for the implementation of national plans.

In Poland in the years 1970–80, the incomes of technical personnel and workers in key industries soared in spite of the warnings of the planners. Paying fictitious overtime to boost the income of the workers, distributing financial rewards for the accomplishment of plans which were not fulfilled (this often meant falsifying the statistics of production), and promotions tantamount to hidden pay rises became an essential part of management policy. This contributed to the growth of pay differentials which were magnified by the common practice of dividing the bulk of the financial bonuses and premiums among managerial staff.

Promotions, some of them fictitious, became one of the main ways of boosting individual incomes. During the decade the number of supervisory posts reached the staggering level of 1 million. In the course of the years 1973–7, about 190,000 new supervisory posts were created, while at the same time the number of industrial enterprises fell by 600, the number of construction enterprises by 185, and the number of independent agricultural syndicates by 5,120. Out of the million individuals in supervisory positions there were 100,000 occupying the posts of chief directors and directors in institutions and enterprises of national importance (*Głos Pracy*, 2 October 1979, and Podemski, 1979).

The steps taken towards decentralisation made bending the rules easier for managers and administrators. Directors in association with chief accountants were able to manipulate pay funds the way they wanted. Local dignitaries overspent the public funds which they controlled. The chairmen of co-operatives allocated special bonuses to themselves and their closest associates. Research teams in scientific institutes demanded money for projects which were often of no value to the national economy and served only to increase the incomes of those who carried them out.

All these practices did not stop after 1976 when symptoms of the economic crisis became obvious. On the contrary, with creeping inflation an ever stronger pressure for pay increases was exercised by groups with a strong bargaining position. A lot of scattered information confirms this widely known tendency. For instance, in 1979–80 some directors of enterprises were granted bonuses in tens of thousands of zloty and more by the planning commissions (Rymuszko, 1981). In a parliamentary speech references to individual incomes in the public sector amounting to 400,000 zloty per year were made, that is, incomes twice as high as those of the highest dignitaries. The malpractices were clearly visible, the redistribution of the national income within the public sector becoming one of the most powerful factors of growing inequality.

GROWING INEQUALITIES IN COLLECTIVE CONSUMPTION

In the nineteen-seventies, public consumption, including funds for social benefits, grew in all Communist countries reflecting growing prosperity and the determination of the governments to improve living standards by spending more on housing, social welfare, health service, nurseries, etc. In Poland, however, expenditure in this area lagged behind the other East European societies (Pohorille, 1979, p.78):

Table 4.3 Social funds as percentage of general consumption in selected countries

Country	1960	1970	1975
Czechoslovakia	29.5	29.9*	30.0
USSR	26.1	31.2	34.9
Hungary	18.8	23.2*	27.3
Poland	18.4	21.6	22.9

*Data for Czechoslovakia and Hungary for 1968.

In Communist countries the social funds are never evenly distributed among the population. On the contrary, their allocation is highly selective. Many services are linked to enterprises (health centres for the employees), to ministries (closed hospitals and sanatoria for some groups of employees) or trade unions (hotels in health resorts, recreational facilities, in some cases sanatoria, etc.). The sectors and branches of industry which are privileged in terms of wage levels and bonuses are also taking a large slice of social funds. These privileges are also extended over some professional associations. The armed forces and the security establishment enjoy special rights which are justified by security reasons (seclusion and segregation) and manifest themselves in maintaining special hospitals, hotels, sports grounds, recreational sites, hunting clubs and transport facilities reserved for the personnel. It is also common practice that high officials and influential figures are able to make use of all the amenities belonging to the most privileged occupational groups.

In Gierek's Poland, all these practices were widespread but the greed of party and state officials was growing with their opulence out of proportion to the general improvement of living standards. Their privileged share of social consumption was obvious to all and expanded at a staggering pace compared with other Communist countries.

The distribution of the general consumption fund in Poland in 1976 was as follows (Pazio, 1979):

12% general consumption (i.e. goods and services which are utilised without affecting individual incomes (transport, roads, public buildings, etc.)

11% specific social consumption (i.e. goods and services which are part of individual consumption like housing, subsidised meals, holidays, etc.)

77% individual consumption.

The utilisation of general consumption funds became in the nineteen-seventies subject to many blatant abuses. In both the capital and the provinces, party and state functionaries competed in extracting funds for the construction of sports centres, hunting grounds, summer houses, and recreation centres for the exclusive use of the bureaucratic élites. The following observation of a Polish journalist about conditions in the Koszalin province could be applied to any other area:

The situation of the health service in the province is appalling: the provincial hospital hardly copes with the intake of patients: instead of 250 patients it had to accommodate more than a thousand. At the same time, the shortages of resources did not prevent building private villas, high office blocks, special town halls and offices for the local authorities. (Piekarska, 1980)

The way in which state-financed benefits operated in favour of the upper crust can be illustrated by the case of the village Abramów made public by Solidarity publications. The village was situated in south-eastern Poland in the Bieszczady mountains where a special microclimate favoured a particularly fine breed of deer. The decision was made to use the area as a hunting ground for dignitaries. In 1968, 3,000 ha were fenced off, and over the next few years this was increased to 7,000 ha. The official reason was that the area was needed by the armed forces for strategic reasons. By 1980, the hunting grounds extended over 60,000 ha and the intention was to expand them further. Buffer zones around the hunting grounds were also fenced off and the families living in these zones were compulsorily resettled; those who complied could move to towns where they obtained a flat immediately, but those who resisted were removed forcibly during the night and dumped in one of the dilapidated houses in the mountains abandoned by the Ukrainian population in the late nineteen-forties and pressure was put on them to stop resisting the compulsory resettlement order. In the 'militarised' zone, shooting lodges were erected and special landing strips for planes were constructed to make access easier for the visiting dignataries.

The practice of occupying sites for hunting grounds, holiday homes and sporting grounds to be used by the privileged few (usually higher officials) was common in the nineteen-seventies. The users of these facilities often had at their disposal special transport facilities and personnel; for the more important ones even airports and special highways and roads leading to remote spots were earmarked.

Unequal participation in the public consumption fund could be observed beyond the domain of direct administrative privilege. For instance, the real beneficiaries of the enormous amounts spent on the improvement of public roads were the private car owners since these sums were not matched by appropriate funding of public transport, which in fact deteriorated in the seventies at an alarming rate. The allocation of places in the best schools and nurseries was heavily biased towards the children of the intelligentsia. Significantly, the utilisation of social funds in industrial enterprises was also uneven. Lidia Beskid found that, apart from expenses on the health service (which indicates indirectly the condition of poor health prevalent among this group) manual workers were getting about 36 per cent less from the social funds than the white-collar workers employed in the enterprises (Beskid, 1978; see also Bogus, 1975).

SUBSIDISED PRICES AND SHOPPING FACILITIES AS A FACTOR OF ECONOMIC EQUALITY

A paradoxical consequence of the subsidised cheap food prices in the seventies was the redistribution of the national income in favour of the better-off who were consuming more of the subsidised products (Mozołowski, 1980a). In 1978 the differences in food consumption between people in the lowest income group (that is, families with a monthly income of 1,700 zloty and less per person) and families with monthly incomes of 4,000 zloty and more per person, were the following.

Table 4·4 Consumption per head of selected food products, 1978

Product	Yearly consumption	
	low-income families	high-income families
Meat (kilograms)	50	81.3
Fruit: 7 fruit products (kilograms)	25	61
Butter (kilograms)	7.5	12
Eggs (number of)	147	248

Source: Bywalec (1980).

According to some other sources, in 1979 the disparity in meat consumption between high- and low-income groups was 3:1, that is, the low-income groups were consuming 35 kilograms per person and high-income groups 105. Whatever figure we accept it is obvious that in view of the heavily subsidised prices of meat and meat products, the better-off got the lion's share of public funds allocated to meat consumption. As the then Polish Prime Minister Babiuch declared in 1980, about 40 per cent of the budgetary expenses of the state were spent on subsidising food, rents, electricity, gas, solid fuel and other goods and services (Babiuch, 1980). He himself argued that these subsidies were often contrary to social justice: for instance, the more spacious the flat occupied by a family the higher the subsidy for their rent and electricity irrespective of the number of people who occupied the flat; at the same time, people living in appalling conditions without water, electricity and other amenities enjoyed few advantages of the subsidies system.

The economic differences between high- and low-income groups were, however, much larger than the difference in purchasing power of their respective wages and salaries, because some groups had access to scarce commodities and services supplied within the public sector.

The uncontrolled, inflationary supply of money, on the one hand, and the policy of maintaining artificially low subsidised prices for many basic goods, on the other hand, caused a permanent and growing imbalance between supply and demand. For a time, foreign imports helped to fill the gap, but once the first difficulties in servicing and repaying the loans became apparent the shortages reappeared and became more acute. After 1976 when imports were reduced shortages were increasing from one year to another. People faced empty shelves in the shops which made any rational spending of their money illusory and compelled them to buy more expensive products—if available—or to pay the even higher free-market price. No wonder that by the end of the decade the problem of empty shops became one of the main subjects of journalistic essays and sociological reports. As a leading journalist noted:

It is no secret that the mood of the population deteriorates or improves corresponding to the state of market supplies: 'supplies' are the magic word which has passed in Poland from the economic vocabulary to everyday speech and refers to everything which is connected with full or empty shelves in shops. (Radgowski, 1977)

On the eve of the strikes in the summer of 1980, the distinguished sociologist Stefan Nowak argued in the *Polish Sociological Bulletin:*

Low degree of fulfilment of expectations concerning the standard of living of a considerable part of the society follows from low incomes and is further aggravated by shortages of consumer goods on the market, typical of the last few years. Combined with the necessity of queueing up in front of shops, the situation brings many people's evaluation of this sphere of problems down to a level which I would be inclined to call 'a critical standard', i.e. generalised, strongly emotionally charged, very negative evaluation of their life situation in toto. . . . Since these demands are perceived as legitimate and people expect the state to satisfy them, these states of tension based on the economic situation of the society tend to assume the character of political tension. (Nowak, 1980)

The worsening supply situation in the late nineteen-seventies increased the economic gap between people in various occupations and places of residence. Now the problem became not so much that of access to expensive and more sophisticated goods but, more and more frequently, that of scarcity of meat and fish, of cheap fashionable garments, of popular books and records, all of which were in great demand and short supply.

Thus with shortages in the market becoming more widespread, consumption depended more and more on the patterns of distribution which favoured some groups, while others were at a disadvantage:

1) Many officials were entitled, or simply had the opportunity, to buy some goods 'at the source', that is, in the factories which produced them or in the warehouses where they were stored before distribution to retail agencies. Some officials were entitled to do their shopping in special sections in the big department stores.

2) Meat was distributed directly to large factories ensuring that some workers and white-collar personnel enjoyed a regular supply of high-quality products in sufficient quantities without queueing, (in some factories members of the managerial staff were allocated food products of higher

quality than ordinary workers).

3) Highly industrialised regions were favoured by getting supplies of many products at the expense of the less developed provinces. For instance, in the industrial provinces the yearly meat supplies amounted to 70 kilograms per head (Warsaw and Katowice) while in others like Białystok or Suwałki they were only 17 kilograms per head of the population.

4) Butchers, managers of restaurants, sanitary inspectors, shop assistants, chairmen of agricultural co-operatives, enterprising lorry drivers transporting food were also the beneficiaries of the 'shopping facilities', as well as their friends, relatives and those acquaintances to whom they were prepared to grant favours in exchange for reciprocal services.

Thus, the access to scarce products was becoming a substantial, and sometimes the major component in the standard of living of many groups of the population, whose nominal incomes were otherwise equal. The 'shopping facilities' also boosted extra incomes in the process of swapping goods and services and created a new stratum of the 'haves' cutting across official pay differentials and occupational income differences. The purchasing power of the money of those people who enjoyed the 'shopping facilities' was greater because they could buy what they wanted cheaply, without much delay and of a quality often inaccessible in the official market. Moreover, for many people, access to scarce goods meant the possibility of reselling them at free-market prices. Buying goods at state-controlled prices and reselling them in the inflationary free market became one of the most profitable operations. Shop managers, shop assistants, wholesalers, were in a most beneficial strategic position by being able to hoard and sell scarce products or to pocket extra 'fees', i.e. bribes from clients who were eager to buy a given product at the official price. In this situation the incomes of some enterprising or 'well-placed' individuals were soaring and their life-styles were characterised by defiant and arrogant opulence which contrasted with the life of people relying on their official incomes.

THE EFFECTS OF ALLOCATION OF FLATS, HOUSES AND CARS IN A DUAL PRICE SYSTEM

The gap between official and free-market prices was particularly wide in respect to flats and houses, building plots and cars, and a multitude of potential candidates were fighting desperately for the chance of having these assets allocated to them at the low official price.

The high and growing demand for housing clashed with the declining output of the construction industry which had become one of the most conspicuous examples of the violation of the 'law of proportionality' in economic development. Modernisation consisted in replacing traditional methods of building with 'house factories' which produced houses in mass from prefabricated blocks, but the capacity to erect walls and roofs was not matched by the capacity of doing all the complementary work necessary in order to make the buildings habitable. As a result, the house-factories had a surplus capacity which could not be utilised, thousands of blocks of flats remained unfinished, the rate of completion of flats declined and the costs of construction dramatically increased. All this happened at a time of rapidly rising demand for housing because the birth peak cohorts of the nineteen-fifties were reaching adulthood and a massive migration from the countryside to the cities took place. The desperate shortage of accommodation fuelled the competition for flats and the private market prices of housing were soaring.

The difference between the official and free-market prices increased even further the pressure on public housing resources. A chance of having a flat allocated in a tenants' co-operative meant acquiring it for a fraction of the free-market price, hence everybody tried to join the co-operatives even if he had other ways of solving his housing problem (private purchase, inheritance, marriage with a flat owner, etc.).

In the fierce competition for natural assets allocated at state prices the odds were naturally in favour of people in official positions, that is, the party and state bureaucracy and those with the right connections. It should be realised that these opportunities were also exploited for the benefit of children and relatives. Hence the number of would-be candidates for state subsidised 'bargains' was considerable among the most privileged and well-off groups, and the system of allocation was a source of wealth for themselves and their offspring.

The inflated free-market prices of flats are reflected in the sums demanded from foreign-currency buyers by the foreign trade organisation in charge of this kind of transaction.

Table 4·5 Price of 1 square metre in BHZ (Office of Foreign Trade)

Year	Cost in dollars	Cost in 000s zloty
1960	50–60	not available
1975	109	6.3
1976	167–185	10–13.5
1979	164–218	12.8–17
1980	205–230	16–17
1981	240–250	19–19.5

Source: Polityka, 3 January 1981.

These were prices set by the state. The prices in zlotys applied to those Polish citizens who were prepared to pay 30 per cent of the price in foreign currency.

Table 4·6 Free-market prices per 1 square metre in zlotys

Year	Price
1975	8–12,000
1979	20–28,000
1982	32–47,000

These prices should be compared with the official price paid by the members of the co-operatives, which did not amount to more than one-third of the free-market price and could be paid by instalments over a very long period of time.

As long as people who were allocated new quarters had to give back their previous accommodation to the housing authority or housing association, the differences between the official and free-market prices were relevant only for those who had enough means to buy them—if necessary—on the private market. (Very few were the owners of other flats or houses, which they could sell while moving to the flat allocated to them.) Under Gierek, however, it became common practice for dignitaries to dispose of their previous dwellings whatever way they liked. Many vacated their old flats or villas for new ones, leaving the old quarters to their children, some did not hesitate to sell their old flats in the private market or to sub-let them.

The facilities open to some groups in the housing market and the growing difficulties of the average citizen in obtaining accommodation were quite evident. People who had the know-how and were able to pull strings received the lion's share of the decreasing numbers of new housing stock. A considerable number of flats built by co-operatives and subsidised by the state were arbitrarily allocated to employees of the state administration, and to the managerial élite without much concern for the members of co-operatives who had been waiting for many years for a flat of their own.

In 1966–70, members of the co-operatives received 66 per cent of the flats built by the co-operatives, but in the years 1971–5, their share fell to 54 per cent and, from 1976–80 to 38 per cent. The number of fully paid-up members waiting for flats for three or more years went up from 0.4 million in 1970 to 1.6 million in 1980 (Żarski, 1981).

New housing construction lagged far behind natural population increase because more and more resources were absorbed by accelerated industrialisation and all sorts of public buildings. The gap between the number of households and the number of flats from 1970 to 1978 grew as follows (Żarski, 1980):

	1970	1978
Households in thousands	9,376	10,948
Flats in thousands	8,081	9,326

In 1970 there were, as we see, 1.16 households per flat, while in 1978, in spite of massive construction of new buildings, the ratio exceeded 1.17. It should also be noted that the policy of neglecting modernisation and maintenance of existing housing stock contributed to the rapid deterioration of the houses, many of which had been erected before the Second World War, or shortly after 1945 when the quality of construction was very low.

A journalist found that in Cracow an average family had to wait for about ten years for a flat: he presented the case of a university don who had been living in a university hostel with his wife and son for seven years: his flat consisted of one small room and a bathroom which, late in the evening, was used as a study or a place for entertaining friends (Strzała, 1979).

The appalling housing conditions of many families contrasted sharply with the sumptuous office buildings mushrooming in all cities, beautiful houses erected for the local officials, new estates belonging to people with money and decent blocks of flats built by privileged industries and institutions for their employees.

In the case of cars, a cherished possession in very short supply, the difference between the official and free-market prices also became a source of social privilege and financial gain. Those who were able to get vouchers entitling them to purchase a car at the official price were saving or gaining hundreds of thousands of zlotys: a car bought for an official price of 150,000 zlotys could be worth three times as much in the free market. By reselling it after two or three years for the same or a higher price (a paradoxical price structure for used cars in the free market), an individual who was able to avail himself of the car voucher privilege again, could not only cover the cost of a new car, but also pocket the difference, amounting to one or two years' average salary. While for the man in the street the obtaining of a car voucher was a matter of luck and/or long waiting, many party and state functionaries were able to get such warrants quite frequently and used these facilities in full. Neither in the case of housing transactions, nor in that of cars, were their profits registered in any published statistics.

ACCESS TO FOREIGN CURRENCY

An important source of extra income hardly reflected in official statistics, was access to hard currency. The difference between the official and black-market exchange rates is a phenomenon common to all countries where the local currency is not convertible. In Communist countries these discrepancies are, however, very great, not so much because many transactions involving foreign currency are illegal, but because dollars and other foreign currencies can buy goods, often unobtainable in any other way, including necessities such as medicines, and luxuries such as fashionable clothes, high-quality cars or holidays abroad.

The discrepancy between the official and black-market exchange rates gives enormous profits to holders of foreign currency. A mere sum of thirty dollars sent by a relative from the USA or saved during an official trip abroad, exchanged by a 'private dealer', assured in Poland a sum equivalent to one-and-a-half times the monthly average salary in 1978. People who were receiving pensions from abroad, had royalties paid in foreign currency, or were travelling to the West on a foreign or local grant, as well as those engaged in hard-currency deals in Poland (including prostitutes operating among foreigners), were easily acquiring disproportionately large sums of money. Some of them accumulated real fortunes exceeding anything which could be earned or saved by the average employee in Poland.

In the nineteen-seventies the development of trade relations with the West, and the huge influx of money from abroad, gave many individuals access to hard currency on a scale hitherto unknown. State officials enjoyed more generous travel allowances than ever before, commissions and gifts from foreign business partners became a standard practice tolerated by the state, restrictions relating to the possession of foreign currency were lifted, permits to travel abroad were usually granted (provided there were no serious political reservations) and regulations were issued restricting the rights of customs officers to search the luggage of party and state officials returning from abroad. The Polish authorities, short of foreign currency, encouraged the owners of foreign currency to deposit their money in freely accessible, interest-bearing bank accounts. They were assured that, in doing so, no one would ask questions about the source of their hard-currency funds. The black-market rates for hard currency were virtually legalised by Polish banks which awarded 'loans' against the equivalent in foreign currency.

As we have said, some of these benefits of access to foreign currency were significant in Poland in the late nineteen-fifties and the nineteen-sixties, but in the decade of the nineteen-seventies the sheer expansion of these phenomena was enormous. This was reflected in the growing number of people who, in view of the amount of foreign currency in their possession, qualified—if their riches were expressed in Polish zloty—as millionaires and multimillionaires, a million zloty being the equivalent of 4,000 dollars or of eighteen years of average earnings in 1978.

THE IMPACT OF THE UNREGISTERED ECONOMY ON THE REDISTRIBUTION OF NATIONAL INCOME

Some people employed in the public sector were able, as we have said, to draw extra benefits from their position, be it as officials with a foreign-currency income, as shop assistants taking 'fees' for selling goods from 'under the counter', or as dealers in scarce commodities. On top of that, many state employees were making money by charging their clients for services they were supposed to provide within their working schedules. Doctors who took money from their patients for treatment within the health service system, for placing them in public hospitals, and for operations carried out in these hospitals, were the most common example of this phenomenon. Nurses expected money for their help in the wards, charwomen demanded payments for performing necessary chores, hospital porters expected tips for bringing letters and flowers from relatives and friends to the patients. In state-owned garages, mechanics took extra money for a decent overhaul of cars, tailors working for co-operatives pocketed private payments for garments cut and made in the workshops, and building and maintenance workers did odd jobs for the tenants in blocks of flats, using stolen materials and carrying out their commissions .in normal working hours.

At all levels, and in a variety of forms, the exchange of services for money was taking place, and many a state employee was earning from extra sources much more than a ministerial salary. A most important element of the parallel market was the acquisition by registered and unregistered private entrepreneurs (including farmers) of goods and services they needed for the normal conduct of their business from enterprises owned by the state or controlled by local authorities—transactions which usually boosted the incomes of all involved.

The phenomena just described are common to all Communist countries but in Gierek's Poland they grew out of all proportion because of the relaxation of discipline, the pressure of the private sector, the great amount of money in the hands of many occupational groups who were the consumers of privately produced goods and services, and the complacency of all who expected profits from deals of the kind discussed above. This complacency characterised even militiamen and state officials who were supposed to control illegal activities.

It should be noted that all these extra profits were essentially tax-free. While the number of registered private craftsmen remained more or less stable, a large and growing number of 'cowboy' entrepreneurs and traders without any overhead expenses or financial risk embarked on all sorts of unofficial ventures and transactions. Indirect evidence of this trend was the number of cars acquired and homes built in the last decade by families whose official incomes could in no way cover such expenses and expensive trips abroad booked by individuals whose salaries were below the national average.

The system operated in such a way that in many cases private market prices were based on the monopolistic position of the dealers, suppliers, or producers.

As Professor Tymowski (1979) noted, many private

entrepreneurs were able to maintain excessive prices for their goods or services because they were able to monopolise the field. A garage owner who was the only one servicing private cars, or a shopkeeper selling certain brands of foreign goods without any competition in a particular region, were free to establish prices as high as some people were prepared to pay. The policy of the authorities to restrict the expansion of private business and to limit the number of private establishments, protected the monopolistic position of the few who had succeeded in establishing themselves once and forever. The shortages and the rapidly declining value of money contributed to the inflationary prices as well—some people were virtually indifferent to the price if they only could convert their depreciating zlotys into some marketable goods.

The differentials within the officially registered private sector in towns were considerable. On the one hand, small craftsmen subject to harsh taxation and trying to keep their books in order found it difficult to make both ends meet especially if they were not prepared to buy raw material from illegal sources. On the other hand, enterprising businessmen, and especially those who knew how to pull strings and did not hesitate to keep double accounts, were able to make quick and enormous profits.

Differentials were also growing in agriculture where the gap between the rich and the poor increased in line with the inflationary increases of private-market food prices and the modernisation of many farms.

ECONOMIC STRATIFICATION

In spite of numerous studies of social stratification in Poland, carried out by individual sociologists and whole research teams, relevant data on income differentials, which would account for all aspects of real incomes, as discussed above, are scarce and often unreliable.

One of the few important studies of economic stratification was carried out by the Polish Institute of Marxism-Leninism in the late nineteen-seventies. A poll was taken in which people were asked to assess their own economic position. The findings were as follows (Sufin, 1980):

Group 1:
9–10 per cent of the polled population
23.6 per cent among the workers, and 9.6 per cent among the intelligentsia

People living at the *minimum level*, i.e., with a monthly income of about 2,000 zloty per head for members of a family and 2,500 zloty for single people. The income would allow them to satisfy elementary material needs only. 'We have enough money to buy the cheapest clothes and food.'

Group 2:
50 per cent of the polled population
41 per cent among the workers and 37 per cent among the intelligentsia

People living on a primary/elementary level which allows them to satisfy a limited range of needs. 'We live very economically to save for more important purchases.'

Group 3:
26.5 per cent among the workers and 36.6 per cent among the intelligentsia

People living on the level of relative affluence, i.e., those whose level of consumption allows them to satisfy a wide range of needs. According to GUS, the Central Statistical Office, the average income for this group for 1978 was 4,500 zloty per head monthly. Flexibility of expenses can be achieved and durable products and trips abroad can be afforded on condition of systematic saving. 'We live economically and have all we need.'

Group 4:
6.6 per cent among the workers and 12.7 per cent among the intelligentsia

People on the highest level of affluence. They are able to satisfy all their needs and have a wide freedom of choice. Their standard of consumption includes luxury goods. 'We have enough without any need to economise.'

These data must be read with caution: they are based on 'self-assessments'; the economic position of the respondent is not measured against fixed criteria but is evaluated in terms of his own aspirations and the needs regarded as legitimate among different social groups. The findings that 6.6 per cent of the workers are placed in the highest bracket sheds light on the far-reaching inconsistencies inherent in the chosen method. There is no doubt that the most successful and best-paid manual workers did not usually avail themselves of luxuries enjoyed by many affluent groups in Poland. Sumptuous villas, luxuriously furnished with foreign-made furniture and fittings, could hardly ever be seen in housing estates inhabited by affluent factory workers, and the same is probably true of summer houses and dachas in fashionable health resorts and beauty spots. The same can be said about sending children to foreign schools and universities, collecting antiques and *objets d'art*, and spending money in exclusive restaurants, entertaining business friends, or building up lucrative business ventures for one's children. Unfortunately, all these aspects of the quality of life of some groups, in contrast to that of others, have been utterly neglected by students of Communist societies.

A rather impressionistic, but fairly sound assessment of economic stratification in Poland has been presented by the journalist, E. Skalski, who has distinguished:

1) An 'aspiring' group, i.e., people who were subject to all sorts of shortages and wanted desperately to have access to more products and services which were beyond their reach. They rejected the traditional policy of resignation and restraint and wanted a change in their status, without much chance of achieving it.

2) An 'advancing' group, i.e., people having enough money to buy goods and services of higher quality, but at the cost of many restraints and stresses; a good and fairly typical example is a family which puts all its savings into buying a car they can hardly afford to maintain.

3) A 'satisfied' group, i.e., people who own what they want. A large part of this group is under constant stress knowing that the source of their incomes is not legitimate, and feel ostracised because of their conspicuous consumption (Skalski, 1979).

As long as the national income was increasing, these economic differences could be tolerated. The situation changed dramatically, however, when the growing crisis resulted in drastic shortages and inflationary price increases.

The two levels for meat prices were the best example of how inflation worked against the poorer section of the population and, at the same time, how unreliable were the statistics which determined the economic differentials on the basis of low prices. The official low prices of meat were maintained, but meat was in most cases unavailable in the normal shops though it could be bought in the so-called 'commercial' shops at a much higher price, or at an even higher price in the private market.

The workers who revolted against the price increases in 1976 won their point, but the economic situation of many of them became worse than before. It was also after the events of 1976 that they realised that they were the main victims of an inefficient economy and incompetent management. While their economic situation gradually deteriorated, the managerial staff and the bureaucratic élites seemed to grow more and more prosperous. The rapid decline in the construction of new flats, the drastic deterioration in the functioning of overcrowded schools and nurseries, the growing difficulties of the public transport system and the shortage of drinking water in many cities contrasted with the building of new luxury hotels and restaurants, the construction of new public buildings for party committees, militia headquarters or managerial conference halls.

Inequalities in health service facilities seemed most staggering. The situation became dramatic in the late nineteen-seventies when the growing shortage of hard currency brought about drastic cuts in the purchase of drugs abroad, and when hospitals for ordinary patients—as distinct from the privileged establishments—experienced shortages of basic instruments and materials. As one of the respondents quoted in the reports on Poland noted: 'There are hospitals that are so poorly supplied, they do not even have cotton wool, and our relatives die lying in the corridors; but other hospitals are equipped with private rooms and full medical care for each room' (*Poland*, 1981, p.62).

The authors of the survey mentioned on p.113 (Sufin, 1980) draw our attention to the important trends in economic stratification in the late nineteen-seventies.

According to their findings:

1) There was a downward movement of the moderately well-off groups towards groups located on the 'primary' level.
2) A regression of the people living on the primary level, towards the lowest, i.e. the mere substance level.
3) A slowing down of the upward movement of groups living at the subsistence level.
4) An increasing number of people enjoying the higher levels of affluence.

The trend just described consisted, then, of a widening in the gap between the rich and the poor following the erosion of the real incomes of the low-income groups.

The numerous opinion polls carried out in the late nineteen-seventies, and in 1980–1, clearly show that the public rejected the growing inequality in living standards. The sharpest opposition was aroused by inequalities due to positions of privilege and the differences between people in supervisory posts and rank-and-file employees.

Professor Malanowski (1981), referring to the public opinion poll carried out in September and October 1980, quotes the following figures which illustrate the perception of inequality in Poland:

55 per cent of people believe that inequalities are *very great*.
30 per cent believe the inequalities to be *great*.
6 per cent think the inequalities are *small*.
4 per cent regard the inequalities as *negligible*.

Jan Malanowski comments that the very high percentage of respondents taking an extreme point of view is significant, since in normal conditions people would be inclined to cluster around the moderate opinions.

People were also asked which groups in Poland have been unfairly treated, that is, where the principles of social justice were violated. The answers were the following (ibid.):

Percentage of respondents	Groups indicated as unfairly treated
34%	the poor compared with people having money
47%	rank-and-file employees compared with people in high position
34%	non-party members compared with party members
33%	the uneducated compared with the educated
26%	manual workers compared with non-manual employees
23%	people living in villages compared with people in towns

As far as privileges were concerned, 66 per cent of respondents protested against privileges relating to occupational and administrative positions. The following privileges were particularly identified (ibid.):

— too high remunerations
— access to scarce goods (flats, cars)
— the use of special distribution centres (special shops)
— better social benefits, such as luxurious rest homes and holidays abroad

Opinions about differentials in salaries were distributed in the following way:

86 per cent regarded the differences as too great
4 per cent regarded the differences as proper
3 per cent regarded the differences as too small

Source: 'Nierówności i niesprawiedliwości społeczne w świadomości spoleczeństwa polskiego', an OBOP & SP survey held at the end of September and the beginning of October 1981 covering a representative sample of the Polish population.

All these findings show clearly that the growth of economic differences under Gierek's regime brought about the alienation of the under-privileged majority, even if many of them thought that, on balance, their economic situation somehow improved in the seventies. The following table summarises overall feelings on the subject.

*Table 4·7 Subjective assessment of family living conditions in the
1970s (Question: 'Taken overall, did your family's living conditions
improve over the years 1970–8?')*

Social category	Improved considerably	somewhat	Remained unchanged	Deteriorated somewhat	considerably	Other
Economically active						
total:	11.2	52.3	22.1	9.2	3.1	2.1
Workers	6.6	51.6	26.5	9.2	3.4	2.1 ·
Intelligentsia	16.8	50.3	18.3	7.3	4.0	2.7
Peasants	11.7	56.7	17.2	10.3	2.7 ·	2.3
Peasant-workers	11.2	52.7	25.4	8.3	1.8	1.4
Pensioners	9.0	37.4	27.0	18.4	6.0	2.2

Source: Beskid (1980), p.142.

But the apparent discrepancy between the findings that the
majority of the population thought their living conditions
had undergone, at least, some improvement and the strong
opinions with regard to social inequality can be explained by
the difference in the time the respective polls were taken. It
should be especially noted that in 1979 and 1980 there was
an alarming deterioration of the economic situation and the
living standards of the population. Moreover, the shortages
in the provision of medicines and medical equipment
reached such an alarming point that public appeals were
made abroad for help. Indeed, the most conspicuous feature
of the last two to three years before the 1980 upheaval was
the extreme increase of social inequality which had become
more obvious than ever before: all observers witnessed a
display of wealth at a time when the overall economic
situation was rapidly deteriorating.

ECONOMIC INEQUALITY AND THE STATE OF ANOMIE

All attempts to quantify the growth of social and economic
inequality in Poland are limited by the lack of reliable
statistics relating to the wealthiest strata in society. In their
pursuit of the 'averages' and lack of interest in the extremes
(Professor Tymowski was a rare exception in this respect),
Polish sociologists studying social stratification disregarded
the relatively small, but socially very significant, group of
very rich people, whose conspicuous consumption did much
to intensify the dissatisfaction of the average Pole with his

living conditions—an ostentation incompatible with the reticence which veiled the sources of income of the new wealthy minorities.

There is no doubt that a considerable part of the material affluence was due to growing corruption—we shall deal with this issue in respect of bureaucratic élites in the next chapter. However, the widespread incidence of corruption must not distract our attention from the new economic mechanisms at work, which made more people rich while at the same time eroding the economic position of the masses. As we said before, these mechanisms were manifest in the redistribution of public funds in favour of the 'haves', the growing depletion of the official market, and the growing circulation of many commodities in the parallel market. People who were able to buy goods cheaply were by this very fact in a privileged position, and even more so if they could resell some of these goods at free-market prices. The dual-price system and the growing shortages multiplied profits based on the circulation of foreign currency—the army of middlemen in all sorts of market transactions grew and the possibilities of earning extra in the unregistered economy were rapidly expanding.

The dual market, dual currency, dual level of incomes— these were the characteristic features of the economy under Gierek. The specific combination of the market with the command economy reinforced inequalities, by allowing many of those who gained disproportionate profits in the secondary market to take advantage of the cheap labour force and cheap, heavily subsidised products available on the official market.

In these circumstances, the link between the individual input of labour and occupational achievements and qualifications was to a great extent disrupted and the differentiation based on the above-mentioned economic mechanisms cut across social strata and occupational groups. The feeling of relative deprivation was therefore running high and no one seemed satisfied with his lot. Workers could see their former colleagues who had become shop assistants, or who worked in the transport of food products, becoming opulent within a few years. Engineers working for state enterprises compared their economic position with fellow engineers working on foreign contracts, a modest official could impress his colleagues and superiors by displaying riches acquired by his wife who ran a shabby boutique with fashionable dresses, and young students determined to make money by doing odd jobs abroad during their holiday trips were earning, in a few months, more than many of their professors could save in years.

Such a situation has been identified by sociologists as a state of utter anomie, that is, conditions in which the whole system of standards and expectations is in disarray, and people are no longer able to make a realistic assessment of their needs, their legitimate aspirations and the ways of satisfying them.

The standards of consumption displayed by the wealthiest strata resembled the standards of the affluent middle classes in Western countries, and yet they became a model and a target of aspiration for everybody who wanted a 'decent' life. These standards were made respectable by the state-controlled media, even if lip-service was paid to the disapproval of 'excessive consumerism', allegedly commended to the Poles by Western propaganda. While these standards were legitimised and widely advertised, it became practically impossible to reach them through hard work and professional achievement. The cult of 'wheeling and dealing' grew but, paradoxically, it would seem, the wealth acquired by the 'wheeler-dealers' was not acceptable by the public as legitimate and well-deserved. The belief that honest, hard-working people could not expect much in life was widespread and accounted for the growing frustration of the younger generation faced with a decrease of the number of well-paid jobs available for them, the prospect of waiting ten to twenty years for a flat of their own and a growing shortage of consumer goods at prices they could afford.

Sociologists have pointed out that most people, when assessing their economic position, accept as a reference group other people very close to them in occupation, living standards and life-style, an attitude which makes the definition of one's own situation and aspirations much more realistic. In Poland in the late nineteen-seventies all such criteria were virtually destroyed, since those who acquired wealth belonged to all ways of life and all occupations. A typical case is that of a worker who visited his *emigrée* mother every two years as he was entitled to, and, working as a builder, brought back over 1,500 dollars every time: he was a rich man not only by comparison with his fellow-workers who did not have relatives abroad or were less enterprising, but could be much better off than his manager, the family doctor or the local party secretary. A dishonest lorry driver transporting meat to shops and selling part of it on his own account, could earn in a few days more than a highly-qualified university don earned in a month. The same applied to a cloakroom attendant in a popular café receiving high tips or a young engineer using his car as an unlicensed taxi in his spare time.

Although economic inequalities cut across different classes and occupational groups, some groups had a statistically better chance of becoming better off than others. However, since most benefits were not automatically linked with one's status but depended on using the opportunities offered by one's position, the feeling of relative deprivation was fairly common even among the well-endowed groups where some members had much higher living standards than others.

The economic decline made this situation even worse because the empty shops and soaring private-market prices made people realise that the salaries and wages they had regarded as satisfactory a relatively short time earlier were not sufficient to secure their accustomed living standards. For those on fixed salaries and wages, lacking the opportunity of increasing their income, such changes constituted a severe disadvantage. Even those with relatively more money found that there was not much their money could buy at official prices and was not sufficient to avail themselves of the private market; hence the trend to enforced savings, the value of which was rapidly declining.

PREMATURE CONSUMERISM?

The ethos of socialism in the Soviet sphere was for a long time that of an ascetic producer who lives very modestly and is prepared to sacrifice his well-being, and even that of following generations, for the benefit of society.

Although Gomułka criticised this ethos as a remnant of the Stalinist past and declared that the main aim of the Polish United Workers' Party was to improve the living standards of the population, he insisted that society must live within its means, and preached modesty and restraint in the satisfaction of material needs.

Gierek represented a completely different philosophy. He was undoubtedly instrumental in establishing a consumer society which was welcomed by all social groups as a model for a better quality of life. A contented consumption-orientated citizen was, for the leadership, the model of a socialist man, who works hard and obeys his superiors provided he is well paid and able to satisfy his growing needs in a well supplied market. Technological advance was to provide the answer to the problem of how to satisfy consumers' expectations. In the province of Katowice, which for many years was Gierek's fief, practice seemed to confirm the success of the model of socialist man.

Those who believed that Gierek's emphasis on consumption would solve the country's political problems did not realise that the privileges enjoyed by the inhabitants of the mining districts were, to a great extent, based on the uneven distribution of funds, goods and services. The miners were not only among the best paid workers, but the districts in which they lived enjoyed higher supplies of food products and industrial goods than other areas, higher funds for social facilities and a more generous allocation of productive capacities for the building of houses.

For many years, people used to travel to Katowice to buy certain goods which were not readily available elsewhere. Workers and young graduates who looked for well paid jobs settled down in Silesia in the hope of getting good money and generous perks, including flats in housing co-operatives or in estates built by the enterprises. It is very likely that Gierek and his followers genuinely believed that once they adopted the same policy of promoting consumerism on a national scale, the whole of Poland would resemble affluent Silesia, and in the same way as they had previously used central Polish funds to benefit the miners, they turned to foreign loans to increase general living standards.

In 1970 Poles did not accept Gierek in the same enthusiastic way as they had welcomed Gomułka in 1956, but they supported his programme of building 'a second Poland' and quickly warmed to his policy of consumerism. In the first few years there were surprisingly few critics of Gierek's strategy among professional economists, the intellectuals supported it, and party activists endorsed his policy without any reservations.

Consumerism as an ideology was generally accepted. In this respect there was a striking similarity between Poland and all other countries of the Eastern bloc. The vision of a 'second Poland' with ever-rising living standards and a totally modernised economy was captivating and gave Gierek the kind of legitimacy which helped to cover up for the basic shortcomings of the system. Indeed, features of the system frowned upon by the public did not change: the arbitrary rule of the party–state bureaucracy could hardly be justified were it not for the economic perspectives they presented to the public. Consumerism operated thus as a new form of political ideology, as the regime's principal trump card where other arguments failed.

At the same time, as the public opinion polls indicate, consumerism became a psychological fact. People believed that the economic situation would improve from one year to another, that economic growth was possible and was bound to bring better living conditions for everybody.

This belief was reinforced by the prevailing myth of Western opulence which ignored the gravity of the problems and difficulties in the most affluent societies and failed to recognise the new issues faced by the economy in the most advanced countries.

As Portes (1978, p.85) commented: 'If the population are still dissatisfied after five years of per capita real income increases at 9.5 per cent per annum, as indeed they appear to be, it is hard to see what will or could satisfy them.'

Some observers drew from the rising expectations of the Polish population the conclusion that the roots of the explosion of 1980 are to be sought in 'premature consumerism'. The state, they argue, was not able to offer the Polish people what they wanted and the frustration of the workers who expected from the state too much too soon was the major reason of their rebellion against the system.

This explanation plays down the real development of the economic situation in the nineteen-seventies when the economic imbalance was growing. Not only were the hopes of the workers for further improvements in their living standards not satisfied, but the economic situation of the masses was rapidly deteriorating—best documented in the official information about the development of strikes in 1980. The available evidence points to shortages and price rises as the source of dissatisfaction, not to frustrated hopes of a consumer paradise. In nationwide opinion polls carried out in 1977 and 1979, over 70 per cent of the respondents complained about shortages of many commodities and demanded the introduction of meat rationing (Sufin, 1983). In 1979, white-collar and manual employees in 164 enterprises were asked what kind of a pay rise would secure them a decent living standard. The average desirable increases which were computed from the responses of technical personnel amounted to a 46 per cent rise in salaries and 64 per cent rise in income per person; the workers wanted their wages to be higher by 48 per cent and incomes per person by 81 per cent (Sufin, 1983). These figures may not have indicated exactly what people realistically expected, but they undoubtedly reflected the growing concern with rising prices and the staggering cost of commodities available only in the private market.

By 1975–6, the queues for food and other essentials were long and annoying (see Jurcan, 1980), but by the end of the nineteen-seventies they were becoming a nightmare. At that time, shortages in supplies of basic products grew out of all proportion (although later on worse was to come). In March 1979 the Ministry of Internal Trade listed 280 products for which demand was difficult to satisfy and the list grew longer in the following year.

In pharmaceutical supplies the situation was critical. Many small factories were liquidated for the sake of modernisation, easy credit encouraged the import of essential medicines, the large modern enterprises disregarded the essential needs of the home market; when, along with other cuts, the imports of pharmaceutical goods were drastically reduced there were shortages of many important products, including aspirins and other analgesics, sanitary towels, syringes, anti-depressant drugs, vitamins, the main drugs used to treat heart disease, etc. etc.

Table 4·8 Time spent by an average family on shopping

Year	1966	1969	1970	1971	1975	1976
Minutes per day	63	87	94	73	94	98

Source: 'Raport doradców', *Polityka*, 29 November 1980.

The effects of pollution and lack of funds for labour protection and safety became staggering. According to the data for 1980, only 12.5 per cent of people who were pensioned off in the Lenin Steelworks in Cracow got normal retirement pensions, while 80 per cent were awarded invalid rents (S.C. Biedni ale zdrowi, 1983). As the report, *The State of the Republic* stated:

The sorry state of the food market has created a situation in which ever greater numbers of the population get inadequate nutrition. In view of progressive inflation, this situation is bound to get worse. Considering that the greater part of the population growth in our country comes from families with the lowest standard of living, it is not far-fetched to say that this constitutes a real threat to the nation's health. It is worth pointing out that according to research done by health and epidemiological authorities, 25 per cent of the food products on sale have characteristics that are to some degree harmful to health, to say nothing of the many food products that are commonly adulterated by producers. . . . In situations of chronic, serious food shortages, the steady spread of alcoholism seems especially threatening. . . . We should . . . look into why people are drinking more, why alcohol is the only consumer product on sale virtually all day, and why we have thirty times as many liquor shops as Sweden. (Poland, 1981, p.88)

All these facts cast light on the nature of discontent with the economic situation in the seventies and disprove the theory of premature consumerism. As in the early fifties (the period of the Six-Year Plan) the Polish population faced a rapid deterioration of the economic situation. But there were important differences. This time falling living standards were the result of a policy deriving from the desire of the party to achieve a rapid improvement of living conditions. This time also the country was divested of its internal reserves and deep in debt. And finally, this time the impoverishment of many was occurring simultaneously with the enrichment of a few and with the unashamed and defiant display of riches by successful entrepreneurs, crooked operators, corrupt officials, opulent professionals, conmen, and enterprising functionaries in different occupations and stations of life.

5 Bureaucratic corruption in an acquisitive society

Under Stalinist rule, the Communist bureaucracies enjoyed many privileges, ranging from better food in their canteens, higher salaries and special shops, to better flats, chauffeur-driven cars and luxurious holidays in the best health resorts. The same pattern was observed everywhere in East Europe, including Poland, in the nineteen-fifties, when party–state officials began to enjoy better apartments, cars and other privileges linked to their status.

Corruption among party and state officials was undoubtedly quite common under Stalinist régimes, but at that time there were many disincentives which prevented malpractices from spreading. The ideological commitment of the old guard and party zealots in the post-revolutionary years certainly contributed to the 'puritan' ethos of the Stalinist bureaucracy, but many other factors were significant, too.

(1) Under the Stalinist régime, a general feeling of insecurity and fear among the party and state bureaucracy dominated. Constant purges, trials, and witch-hunts made officials cautious and keen to prove their loyalty in every possible way, including shows of austerity and devotion to the Communist cause.

(2) The pattern of life and work imposed by Stalin and exemplified by his own behaviour put severe demands on his subordinates. Long hours of work often extending through the night, a manifest lack of concern for leisure time and holidays, restricted social contact and disapproval of 'petty bourgeois' desires for material luxuries shaped the attitudes of officials faithful to party and state.

(3) The range of goods available in the post-war decades was rather limited. Trips abroad were confined to a narrow circle of functionaries who usually did their best to show their contempt for the decadent West. The choice of commodities which could be acquired for cash was very

limited.

(4) As far as accommodation and some 'consumer durables' were concerned, they could be used but not owned, irrespective of rank and function. Flats were nationalised, private cars were rare, chauffeur-driven limousines belonged to state enterprises and offices, and land could not be acquired by private individuals.

(5) Officials were subject to tight control by security and party organs both in their official and their private lives. There were hardly any places where money could be spent without attracting the attention of the security apparatus; restaurants and hotels were under surveillance all the time, caretakers reported on their tenants, and party comrades were alert for any sign of improper conduct in their friends and even in members of their families.

In these circumstances, ownership of material assets was certainly less important than the chance of enjoying access to these assets by virtue of official status. The quality of life of higher officials was determined by their right to live in spacious flats, to have meals in subsidized canteens, to be able to use cars owned by their institutions, to have rooms in luxurious hotels or sanatoria allocated to them when needed, to be able to have theatre seats booked and to buy in special shops—all these were 'perks' associated with the offices they held.

To conclude, the system protected itself against the excessive greed of state functionaries. The most important advantages were the privileges gained from the holding of official positions in the hierarchy, and were not associated with the individual ownership of valuable material assets.

It should be noted, however, that a certain degree of deviation and even corruption was often tolerated. Stalin himself was known to like to have a hold over members of his apparatus, and enjoyed discovering irregularities and abuses committed by his closest collaborators. He felt more secure for being able to use this knowledge, and considered it necessary to keep his partners and subordinates in constant fear and suspense.

It is interesting to note that, in this system, even the highest party leaders, perhaps more than any others, were deprived of any private assets. After Stalin's death, his daughter had only some money earned by him for his 'literary' activities. Similarly, Bierut's daughters had to live on an average normal income and one of them was helped financially, after her father's death, by an aunt who had some money from a book she had published.

After Stalin's death, things changed considerably both in Russia and in other Communist countries. Bureaucracy recovered from the domination of the dictator and the bureaucrats acquired a security of tenure unknown under Stalin's rule and also gained new privileges.

Grossman (1977, p.36) points to the following factors which contributed to the development of illegal economic activities and corruption in the USSR;

(a) the diminution of terror;
(b) the spread of cynicism about the official economic system and party rule;
(c) the boost to consumer expectations from the successes of the economy in many fields;
(d) the considerable rise in private-car ownership: nearly every aspect of acquisition, operation, maintenance and repair of automobiles was connected with some illegal practice;
(e) the opening of the Soviet Union to foreign trade in both directions;
(f) the rapid expansion of the Soviet merchant marine with the resultant inflow of smuggled goods and currency;
(g) the effect of a sharp increase in the liquidity of the Soviet household.

The impact of these changes on the morale of party and state officials was enormous. Simis (1982) provides ample evidence of how virtually all sections of the administrative and managerial apparatus were exposed to the temptations of illegal earnings in post-Stalinist society.

The stabilisation of the private sector in Poland under Gomułka and the depoliticisation of the economic supervision over state-owned industries created new opportunities for profitable 'transactions' between state functionaries and those prepared to buy economic favours.

The incidence of clearly corrupt practices among lower

and middle-rank officials increased rapidly, but if any such practices were discovered, the culprits were liable to severe punishment.

However, the rapid progress in the scope and variety of corrupt practices under Gierek's regime (as exposed in 1980–1) was spectacular and marked an obvious change in the position of the party–state bureaucracy as compared to the sixties. Referring to bureaucratic corruption in the 1970s, Brus states:

> The ideological and moral degradation of uncontrolled power was combined with increased opportunities for corrupt practices due both to gross imbalances in domestic markets and to the complex temptations of business dealings with the West; the state's desperate scramble for every piece of foreign currency and the resulting semi-legal parallel circulation of Western money multiplied the opportunities for illicit gains. (Brus, 1983b, p.40)

FACTS REVEALED ABOUT CORRUPTION AT THE HIGHEST LEVEL OF THE HIERARCHY IN POLAND

Among people whose malpractices in the holding of property investment were publicly denounced after Gierek's fall we find:
three secretaries of the party's Central Committee; twenty-eight first secretaries of party provincial committees; thirty-four secretaries of provincial committees; seven deputy premiers; eighteen ministers; fifty-six deputy ministers; twenty-one chiefs of provinces and thirty deputy heads of provinces (Obraz tygodnia, *Tygodnik Powszechny*, 12 July 1981).

The scale of corruption can be illustrated by the content of letters received by the Supreme Chamber of Control (NIK) in 1980. The Chamber reported that half of these letters were anonymous. Economic malpractices by party and state officials were the subject of 40 per cent of all these letters (*Życie Warzawy*, 18 March 1981).

Investigation by NIK showed about 50 per cent of the accusations to be true, and reports on letters containing accusations of corruption received by other authorities also showed 50–57 per cent of those accusations to be true.

To put all these figures into perspective, one should remember that leading political figures were among those publicly accused of corruption:

—Gierek himself was accused of buying two houses for a fraction of their real value.

—Prime Minister Jaroszewicz was blamed for hushing up accusations of numerous malpractices involving his son.

—Accusations of various misdemeanours and ordinary crimes were brought against the Ministers of Foreign Trade, Construction, Mining and Finances (two of them committed suicide in 1981).

—Maciej Szczepański, the head of the Television and Radio Office, was arrested in 1980 and put on trial on a charge of several economic crimes, including misappropriation of 1.3 million zloty, and causing losses of 7 milliard zloty (Żurkowie, 1981).

A typical report on investigative proceedings runs as follows (text released by the Polish Press Agency (PAP) in English, 17 March 1981):

Investigative proceedings are currently under way in various parts of Poland against persons responsible for economic abuses and mishandling as well as against those suspected of drawing personal profits from high office held in the state and economic administration. In Katowice, police have launched an investigation into the construction of a road leading to a villa owned by a former minister in the locality of Ustroń. The cost of the project (about 21,000,000 zloty) was met by funds of the State Forest Board in Katowice. The Prosecutor's Office in Wrocław has completed proceedings into the case of the illegal construction, by an industrial construction enterprise in Wrocław, of 14 family houses for people holding various managerial posts in the enterprise and outside it. The houses constructed in the years 1975–7 should not have been built according to the plan, and this prevented the fulfilment of housing construction targets. The same Prosecutor's Office is also conducting an investigation into a case of embezzlement involving 25,000,000 zloty in the Chemitex chemical fibres plant in Wrocław. Police in Warsaw have launched an investigation into the case of an unfavourable contract between representatives of the Varimex foreign trade enterprise and the Polish Optical Works (PZO), and a West German firm. The very terms of the contract, which provided for the production of binoculars, indicated that the PZO could suffer losses of about DM 50,000. Another case currently being investigated by the Warsaw police concerns the conclusion of a contract by the 'Orbis' travel agency under which a Swedish firm has designed and built a recreation centre in Mrągowo. There is evidence that the cost of the centre's construction proved to be 8,000,000 dollars greater than envisaged in the estimate. (Polish Press Agency, 1981)

TYPES OF BUREAUCRATIC CORRUPTION

The disclosure of criminal offences cut across all ranks and sectors of bureaucracy and covered a wide range of illegal practices. The prevailing patterns of bureaucratic corruption were (a) the misuse of state funds; (b) the misappropriation of material resources belonging to the state; (c) the use of unpaid labour; and (d) the falsifying of accounts paid to state enterprises for work done on behalf of private individuals. All of these abuses were linked with the construction of houses, villas and related amenities for, and their acquisition by, party and state officials at a fraction of their real value.

A widely known example of this practice is a housing estate built in Katowice which included houses for Gierek, his son Adam Gierek and the First Secretary of the Katowice Province, Grudzień. Semi-detached houses built for Gierek and other dignitaries in Katowice were financed from funds provided by central and provincial authorities, such as the Office of the Council of Ministers and the Ministry of Construction and Building Materials, as well as the Katowice Provincial Office and several state enterprises situated in the Katowice province.

The houses were officially built for well-deserving miners and veterans in Silesia but only twelve of them obtained flats on the estate.

According to the press reports a second house was built for Gierek in Ustronie Śląskie. According to the official registry document, it was financed by Stanisława and Edward Gierek (⅓), Adam Gierek (⅓) and Jerzy Gierek (⅓) but only Adam Gierek paid 200,000 zloty, the rest was entered as losses for various enterprises. (Żurkowie, 1981).

Another notable example is that of Adam Glazur, former Minister of the Building and Building Materials Industry, who was accused of having paid 340,000 zloty for a house built for him at a cost of 3,000,000 zloty i.e. nine times his contribution (*Trybuna Ludu*, 27 February 1981). Practices of this sort were widespread, and involved party and state functionaries at all levels.

Crimes committed by functionaries at the provincial level reveal the same pattern, with many local dignitaries involved in buying newly built or renovated houses at a fraction of their true value.

The carrying-out of illegal acts of this kind usually involved several steps:

1) Decisions were taken about allocations of building sites usually in very attractive areas. In many cases, plots of land were expropriated from the actual owners under the fraudulent claim that the land was needed for important public buildings. In several cases existing building restrictions were also disregarded.

2) Funds and resources for preparing the sites and erecting the buildings were usually obtained by linking the construction with some large-scale investments for which credits and priorities were already agreed, a practice which obviated the necessity of obtaining the approval of the Central Planning Commission.

3) Once funds and resources were allocated, one (or more) state enterprise was ordered to carry out the work. This usually required such an enterprise to turn its attention from its proper work to the building of residences for high-ranking officials. Since the building of these houses was regarded as having high priority, much extra work and many extra costs were involved.

4) The buildings were usually constructed to a very high standard. Many materials were imported from Western countries and the best craftsmen were employed on the job.

5) In the case of already inhabited houses or flats which were offered to dignitaries, the occupants were resettled irrespective of the cost involved, and without regard to the long lists of people who had been waiting for accommodation for ten or more years.

6) In some cases, officials were able to take possession of several sites and houses, and hand them over to the members of their families. As a rule, officials who were

given new accommodation did not bother to return the old, but kept it to be sub-let at a profit, or offered it to their relatives. The possession of several flats and building sites was regarded as a good investment.

The Secretary of the Central Committee, Ryszard Frelek, owned recreational sites in Serock, Szeroki Bór and Konstancin, and several flats, but in his case, almost all the money owed by him was duly paid, since Frelek had a considerable income from his many publications. (It was commented: 'He did not try to grab anything for himself— he was a solid payer.')

Tadeusz Wrzaszczyk had two recreational sites in Skubianka and Wierzbica, and a villa in Konstancin for which the costs of renovation were covered by the technical section of the Office of the Council of Ministers. The costs were not repaid by Wrzaszczyk. (Żurkowie, 1981).

It should be noted that most malpractices in the building industry involved many officials, whose co-operation in planning and implementing the illegal transactions was necessary. For example: ministers or deputy ministers unofficially initiated or approved a given venture; the heads of state enterprises had to release the labour force and resources for a given job; local party secretaries and local officials were involved in allocating the sites, or in resettling people when necessary; accountants had to present bogus reports to cover up irregularities in spending public money.

In many cases, the building of housing estates for the local population involved the co-operation of many firms and offices. The usual method of securing such co-operation consisted of allocating houses or flats, in the first instance to those directors and officials who were, or could be, of assistance in carrying out the construction. High officials from the respective ministries were also sometimes offered flats or houses on the given site, to secure their support for the project.

Another widespread pattern of malpractice consisted of the allocations of cars, building materials and other equipment by higher officials, including those employed in the Presidium of the Council of Ministers, for personal gain.

Jerzy K. for instance, a former deputy director in the State

Planning Commission, was accused of taking over half a million zloty in return for awarding special vouchers which allowed the recipients to buy cars without delay and at reduced prices. Another employee of the State Planning Commission was charged with receiving 150,000 zloty for the same favour.

A third pattern of corrupt behaviour, widespread among officials employed in foreign trade agencies, was the taking of bribes and gifts from foreign firms for contracts concluded by Poland. The trial of Kazimierz Tyrański, director of the Minex Export–Import Bureau from 1969 to September 1979, revealed the scope of such malpractices. Tyrański was accused of having accumulated 700,000 dollars as commissions paid in return for deals concluded abroad, and in addition he secured 473,370 West German marks, and 311,485 dollars, for his private accounts in West Berlin and Bremerhaven.

Many other deals were probably linked with similar malpractices but the evidence for their occurrence is often not direct; for example, from the mismanagement of many transactions, one could infer that the officials concerned might have obtained private benefits from completing these transactions. It is also characteristic that Polish officials invariably favoured deals concluded in the West for hard currency, over deals with Comecon countries.

CIRCUMSTANCES CONDUCIVE TO CORRUPTION UNDER GIEREK'S RULE

1) The scale and extent of the corruption under Gierek can be at least partly explained as being a reaction to the austere style enforced by Gomułka. Gierek had a reputation as a man of the world, who knew how to enjoy the luxuries of life, and was fully sympathetic to the idea of improving the living standards of people around him.

Gierek, as the powerful First Secretary of Katowice Province was indeed instrumental in the building of many housing estates, many impressive public buildings, swimming pools, sports stadia, etc, in Katowice. He paid great attention to the well-being of party functionaries, and was able to secure for his area a high share of products which were in short supply elsewhere, such as meat, good quality furniture, electrical goods, etc. All this secured him the warm support of the workers and the technocrats.

He was also complacent about 'bending the rules', a practice he had followed in his earlier position. He let the ends justify the means and undoubtedly in this approach he reflected the dominant attitudes among the bureaucracy at large. The whole ethos of Gierek's regime was thus geared towards enrichment and success.

2) The new mood among officialdom can be better understood from the changing composition of the office holders during the seventies. Coming from Silesia, Gierek brought with him many of his former colleagues and protégés whom he trusted and regarded as his closest allies. In Warsaw Gierek might otherwise have felt threatened by the established cliques within the central party and state apparatus. He was also competing with Moczar, who helped him to power after the 1970 riots. By placing his supporters in the highest offices he gained the chance to strengthen his own position. Apart from his Katowice supporters, he also found allies among the *apparatchiki* from Poznań, many of whom he recruited to various offices.

The new officials brought with them other people whom they trusted, and who established, in turn, new networks of protégés in the provinces. There was, as a result, a general increase of mobility in the party–state apparatus, which gave provincial officials the chance to climb up the administrative ladder.

The newcomers from the provinces brought with them a new style of work, and a different lifestyle, in which the cult of private property, material well-being and acquisitiveness was of paramount importance.

3) The administrative reforms of 1975 offered new opportunities for upward mobility in the party–state apparatus. The ranks of higher functionaries employed in provincial offices rapidly swelled when the number of provinces increased from twenty-two to forty-nine.

The chief officials in the newly created provinces expected

to be allocated adequate accommodation, appropriate to their status. They also demanded buildings for offices and other facilities associated with a provincial centre, including newspapers, theatres, law-courts, etc. As a result, corrupt practices among the new dignitaries became commonplace. The provincial leaders were regarded by the central leadership as being under an obligation to arrange things to the satisfaction of the newly appointed functionaries, and this was largely responsible for the sumptuous housing estates and luxurious office buildings erected in towns suddenly promoted to the ranks of provincial capitals. It is thus significant that in most cases the party officials accused of corruption operated either in Katowice or in the newly created provinces.

According to a report by W. Piłatowski (of the Highest Chamber of Control), the first party secretaries of the provinces accused of malpractices were divided into three groups depending on the nature of their activities:

The first group consisted of people who had not paid the full price for summer homes, for flats bought from the state, and for the accompanying technological infrastructure. This applied to secretaries from Zielona Góra, Olsztyn, Bydgoszcz, Poznań, Leszno, Ciechanów, Konin, Ostrołęka, Siedlce and Białystok.

The second group embraced people who built luxury houses or renovated flats to a higher than average standard (Wałbrzych, Bielsko-Biała, Zamość, Płock and Katowice).

To the third group belonged people who were accused of using the resources controlled by them in an uneconomical way, and in making decisions about the construction of educational and recreational centres, sports centres and hunting centres at very high cost (Opole, Kalisz, Przemyśl, Toruń). (Żurkowie, 1981).

4) The administrative reforms also contributed to the weakening of control over local officials, who felt free from close supervision and, as local autocrats, were virtually immune from public exposition or legal prosecution.

5) It should also be noted that Gierek was known to be complacent about the peccadilloes of party and state officials as long as he could rely on their undivided loyalty. He was

prepared to cover up for them, and in most cases also for their offspring.

CORRUPTION AS AN INTEGRAL PART OF THE SYSTEM

The specific circumstances of Gierek's regime are far from being the full explanation of the problem of corruption in Communist Poland. The spread of corruption undoubtedly has its roots in the recent economic and political changes which have been taking place in many Communist countries.

It should first be noted that bureaucratic corruption is by no means a new phenomenon in the Communist East. In the past, however, corruption was restrained by harsh political rule, the nature of the economy and the very privileges which officials enjoyed within the economy. As long as many products and services were simply not available on the open market, officials were less tempted to develop illegal activities, which could jeopardise their careers and the benefits they derived from them.

Control over the activities of the private sector was very tight and had political undertones. An excessive spending of money and a luxurious way of life attracted not only the attention of fiscal officials and the criminal police, but of the security forces as well.

All this has radically changed with the transition, in Poland, to a new type of society which can best be described as the *acquisitive* society. There are several characteristic features of such a society in many countries (although not all). Firstly, there was a growing, even if temporary, affluence which the officials shared with some other groups in society (see chapter 4) and which made conspicuous consumption not only tolerated, but even respectable.

Secondly, there were many more opportunities for making profits out of illegal or semi-legal operations, in conditions of a mixed economy, when the private sector and the black market created innumerable opportunities for a quick profit for dishonest officials.

Finally, there was also a general tendency towards the

legitimisation of the acquisition and accumulation of wealth. The new attitude was partly a reflection of the official policy of activating the private sector and re-establishing the private market as an important part of the national economy. It was also, however, the result of a considerable relaxation of control over consumption, and an indication of moving away from the austerity of the post-revolutionary decades.

In such a system, a good strategic position in the race for the acquisition of goods and services was of primary importance: party and state officials have, in these circumstances, an obvious advantage, and many of them did not hesitate to use it to the full. It is in this context that the growing corruption of the apparatus is to be seen. Salaries became less important than profit-making activities and, among the latter, illegal transactions were certainly the most lucrative.

The post-revolutionary ethos of the party–state bureaucracy reinforced these tendencies. Communist functionaries had become accustomed to being in privileged positions, and sincerely believed that they were among the chosen few who deserved the best society could offer, and much more.

In extending the advantages of their official positions to practices which were illegal, officials were helped by the general habit of bending rules and cutting corners. Since almost all of them did it in the course of their official activities, many of them found it easy to do for their own personal benefit. In an atmosphere of universal deception, that is, falsifying statistics, patching up official reports, and entering fictitious figures in order to obtain extra funds for wages or investments, party and state officials became used to irregularities, and to some extent did not perceive that many of their activities were corrupt.

The question arises: why did the party leaders not try to prevent such abuses of power and corruption? After all, they could have put a stop to individual acquisition based on malpractices, and established new privileges which would have granted the same advantages and benefits in a fully legal way. They probably hesitated to do so because of the possible reaction of the public. At the same time, it was in the interests of the leaders to build up and widen their clientele: corruption made party–state officials dependent individually and collectively on the leadership, and consolidated the solidarity of the élites.

An extract from the Polish press illustrates the tendencies observed above. It summarises the findings of a journalist who followed the activities of J. H., one of the main figures influential in the activities of the Central Radio-Committee (Żurek, 1981).

The author of the article, E. Żurek, notes that at first J. H. led the modest life of a journalist involved in one of the radio programmes. He enjoyed, however, a reputation as a good organiser and, backed by Janusz Wieczorek, then chief of the Cabinet Office, he was appointed General Secretary of the Public Committee of Construction of the Monument of the Child Health Centre. At the same time, he was promoted directly to the position of General Director of Polish Radio.

Within a short time his life changed. He moved from his 'normal' flat into a five-roomed flat (allocated by Wieczorek in his capacity as chief of the Cabinet Office). He was also allotted a large plot of land in Konstancin—a coveted place near Warsaw—where he built a summer home worth approximately 800,000 zloty. He also acquired an expensive car—all this on a monthly salary of 19,000 zloty.

He was arrested on 5 March 1981. Tyrański, himself a major witness for the prosecution in J. H.'s trial, told the interviewing journalist that he had put J. H. in contact with a businessman, Adam Ehrlich, employed by the firm of Freisler-Otis in Austria. Tyrański explained that most firms used to calculate the costs of their orders including commissions/fees for people who were instrumental in placing and arranging the orders.

The career of Tyrański and J. H. is certainly an example of the opportunities created by trade deals with hard-currency countries. Money could be, and was, made by selling official influence and connections. This money could be used abroad, for example for defection, and it could also be kept in foreign accounts, earning interest in excess of anything that could be earned in Poland. There was also a feeling of impunity, provided that the officials who were overstepping their duties were influential enough to stop any criminal investigations.

THE NEW BUREAUCRATIC ETHOS

We have discussed so far the 'logic' of bureaucratic behaviour, regarding the redistribution and re-allocation of surplus products, in terms of the objective factors conducive to acquisitiveness and generating corruption.

The state of 'social consciousness' has to be taken into account as well, if we want to understand the complacency with which the new practices were accepted and promoted by the party–state leadership and, for a considerable time, by the public at large.

There is no doubt that the pursuit of material wealth was a concept deeply embedded in the collective consciousness of a society in which scarcity and permanent want of material goods had become part of everday life. The pursuit of material affluence was thus regarded as perfectly legitimate. Moreover, social tolerance towards illegal activities in general, and in the public sector in particular, was increasing. 'Pinching' things, using official telephones for private conversations, presenting inflated bills for official trips, falsifying reports of output and efficiency, setting up reduced-plan targets to obtain high bonuses and rewards for over-fulfilled plans, were practices widely applied and universally tolerated. The reason for this toleration lay in the conviction that, in a state of permanent scarcity, people were entitled to cope with their problems as best they could, extorting from the state sector what was due to them anyway.

Toleration of and complacency towards the preoccupation with material possessions continued in conditions where living standards had improved considerably, and opportunities for individual accumulation of wealth had increased.

There was, however, another aspect of the collective consciousness which needs more attention—the bureaucratic attitude towards the rules and norms of the system. As we have explained elsewhere, the command economy combined with general scarcity tends to create an inclination to patch up difficulties by an infringement of the rules and by 'pulling strings'. Bureaucratic competitiveness—in the struggle for scarce resources, in securing the labour force necessary for the execution of projects, and in meeting ever-rising economic targets—resulted in pulling strings, cutting corners and using and abusing networks of informal friendships and existing configurations in the hierarchy of power.

These practices invariably generated a contempt for formal rules and regulations. They were regarded as necessary to control other people, especially rank-and-file citizens, but the functionaries regarded themselves as standing above formal constraints and the rule of law. Though others had to obey the rules, they themselves set up the rules, and could circumvent or ignore them if necessary.

In these circumstances, the very notion of what was legal and illegal became obscured and confused. It has been generally assumed that state functionaries who were infringing administrative or legal provisions in order to implement national objectives, should be excused.

In all the practices just described, the dividing line between honest and dishonest public servants was extremely blurred. Even if the honest ones did not abuse the system in order to obtain substantial personal benefits, they were, in many cases, instrumental in helping others to do so, as we have already indicated.

In these circumstances, a peculiar type of normative dualism developed, which helped many to bridge the gap between the prevalent moral standards and the practices which defied them. Many people in official positions agreed that the system, which encouraged bending the rules and stimulated dishonesty was bad and should be radically or gradually changed. At the same time, they would argue, as long as the rules of the game remained unchanged, people had to adjust and to act accordingly. Those who did not, reduced the efficiency of the system and their own chances of organisational effectiveness and individual advancement.

A director who used foreign-currency funds at his disposal

to smooth relations with the respective ministry departments, was thus genuinely helping his enterprise. A chairman of a housing co-operative who allocated flats to local dignitaries in order to secure the allocation of building materials, was seen as following the right path in a difficult situation, even by those who regarded such circumstances as detrimental to society.

This normative dualism led many people to condemn those who, disregarding the rules of the game, were keeping to formal principles and legal acts, irrespective of the chances of success. Such people incurred hostility from their colleagues and superiors, and were often removed from their jobs, accused of lacking a constructive attitude. The accusations were supported not only by officials who could be personally affected by the stubborn obedience to formal principles of their co-workers, but also by those who understood that no particular struggle could change the rules of the game, while a skilful adaptation to them often made it possible to combine individual success with organisational effectiveness and high performance. In other words, the more frequent were irregular practices and circumvention of legal principles, the greater was the pressure on any official who participated in administrative activities to adopt a similar pattern.

Polish society was unprepared to deal with the new situation created by the policies of rapid economic expansion in the seventies when many more functionaries were involved in making important economic decisions and who, while carrying out their functions, were able to divert a greater part of the increasing amount of surplus products to their advantage. There had never been so much money in Poland, there was never such an abundance of raw materials and industrial commodities in circulation, so many new projects set up or so many investments carried out.

In a system in which democratic forms of control were practically non-existent, no effective mechanisms were available to keep the greed and social ill-discipline of the party and state bureaucrats in check.

At the same time, the tax system did not cover the many ways in which private appropriation of the national product could take place. Taxes were geared, from the start, towards entrepreneurs and owners in the private sector, where control was rather strict and complemented by all sorts of extraordinary measures in order to extort as much money as possible from this sector. In the mixed economy promoted by Gierek, these practices were curbed considerably to allow private entrepreneurs to carry on their business, but nothing took their place to control and regulate the incomes of private individuals who were in a position to inflate their earnings through illicit operations.

The very concept of fair progressive taxation generated stubborn resistance. The same applied to the taxation of non-monetary incomes. Renewed attempts to bring them under control were basically confined to individuals in the private sector, while people who received all sorts of benefits because of their official position were getting them virtually tax-free—a situation which in itself became an incentive for rapacious money-making.

The same institutional gap existed in regard to the general rules of conduct of public servants. No attempts were made to register their incomes and material interests, to monitor their 'business' activities, but, on the contrary, any suggestion of doing so would have been regarded by that time as a vote of no confidence in highly respectable public figures.

As a result, an absolute licence permeated all levels of officialdom as far as material acquisitiveness was concerned. The criminal law applied primarily to cases of direct theft, but stopped short of more subtle forms of misappropriation.

The revolutionary past weighed heavily on this complacent attitude. In the system's infancy, party and state officials had been by definition the incarnation of the highest values of the new society, bestowing divine powers on functionaries. Hence their special position defying all forms of institutionalised control. Communists were supposed to be above the law: they were indeed those who were making it. They were unconcerned with the common morality—they decided what was moral and what was not, and sat in judgement over other people, while having supreme power over them. Much of this ethos was retained in circumstances where many of the dignitaries were no more than vulgar thieves and crooks cynically using their position to get the best out of life. Some of them had no illusions themselves about the wickedness of the system they were working for, and were contemptuous of their colleagues who were stupid enough not to use the opportunities open to them.

To conclude, the acquisitive society exemplified in Poland generated corruption of the party–state bureaucracy on a scale previously unknown. It is true that bureaucratic acquisition based on corruption existed from the very beginning of Communist rule but, as we have said, it was limited in scope and character because the bureaucrats were to a great extent restrained, in the early post-revolutionary years, by the nature of the economic and political system within which they operated. In conditions of scarcity and overall shortage, under a system of revolutionary terror and centralised power, the accumulation of material assets was strongly discouraged. Legal restrictions on ownership, the laws of inheritance and a ban on the possession of foreign currency, as well as close political supervision and purges made overt accumulation of wealth virtually impossible.

All these disincentives were removed in a system of relative liberalisation, mixed economy and relative affluence, that is, in conditions in which material acquisition was not only allowed, but even encouraged by the relaxation of restrictions on the possession of material wealth. Flats, houses and other assets increased in value from one year to another, and could be sold in the free market without any of the formal restrictions which were applied under the Stalinist regime, without the penalties of 'capital gains tax' known in Western countries, and without any inquiry into the way they were acquired. Money could be invested in profit-making businesses, allowing the crooks and embezzlers among the bureaucrats to look for alternative ways of making a living than serving the state until retirement. Polish zloty could be changed easily into foreign currency, and transferred in this form abroad, since no one questioned the sources of hard currency paid legally into bank accounts. The accumulation of wealth could become in these circumstances not only an end in itself, but could also be passed on to their children, and open up new life chances.

In the new order of things there was no end to the attempts to acquire material possessions once there were no limits imposed on those material possessions and finance. Party–state functionaries competed in the race for material benefits, and co-operated in eliminating the remaining formal restraints which would prevent them from doing so. The question of who would 'guard the guardians' became more acute than ever since the guardians in this acquisitive society were able to use their power to acquire wealth in every possible way, including legitimised corruption.

This development created a paradoxical situation: the intended improvement in living standards and the relaxation of economic controls became associated with growing abuses and the illegal enrichment of the party–state élites, and eventually generated criticism and moral indignation against the Communist bureaucracy. Legitimised acquisitiveness, which was regarded as a way to social stabilisation, in fact finally destabilised the system. It generated the revolt of the masses, by drawing their attention to the ineptitude of the Communist party in restraining their own ranks from disgraceful pilferage and the misappropriation of the national wealth.

6 Two models of normalisation

The concept of normalisation has been used in connection with political crises in East European countries. Whenever the foundations of the Communist power were threatened by mass movements, as happened in Hungary and Poland in 1956, in Czechoslovakia in 1968 and again in Poland in 1970, one spoke of 'normalisation' to designate the policy which aimed at the restoration of 'law and order'. In plain language, this meant Communist rule.

However, the difference between Gomułka's or Gierek's normalisation in Poland, and normalisation implemented by Kadar in Hungary or Husak in Czechoslovakia, was enormous. In the first case we could speak of *political* normalisation, while the other cases constituted normalisation based on *military intervention* and direct dictatorial rule associated with it.

In a study by Brus, Kende and Mlynař (1982, p.3), normalisation is defined by Zdeněk Mlynař as:

The restoration of a system rejected by the majority of society, at a point when it can be saved solely by the use of large-scale military and political repression. It is motivated by the fear of the Soviet political leadership that without such a forced restoration it will lose its hegemony in the country concerned; the fundamental reason of a military and police intervention as well as of the subsequent 'normalisation' policy is the nature of relations between the countries of the Soviet military-political bloc (the Warsaw Treaty countries).

The authors point out that in all countries in which normalisation based on military intervention took place, there was a common scenario in which the following stages could be distinguished:
(1) First of all a society which had decided to revolt against the Soviet-type system was plunged by the use of the military and the police into conditions visibly worse than those against which it had revolted.
(2) This is followed by a second stage where the defeated

147

must be persuaded that their defeat is irreversible, that
they must capitulate, and that in view of the existing
balance of strength continued opposition will achieve
nothing in the foreseeable future.

(3) Only then is a third stage possible when the victors will
offer certain concessions to the vanquished and begin to
raise hopes that conditions will improve after all, but
only on condition that improvements come from above,
that none of the pillars of the Soviet-type system is
jeopardised, and that Soviet hegemony is secured
beyond the slightest doubt (Brus *et al.*, 1982, p.4).

Let us compare that scenario with what happened in
Poland after 1956 and after 1970. In both cases, a process of
normalisation also followed, but this was achieved by
political and not military means. Thus, the difference could
be summarised as follows:

Aspects of normalisation	Types of normalisation	
	military	political
Ways of dealing with mass upheaval:	Coercion, repressive measures	Concessions to mass demands
Type of leadership:	Nominated	Based on popularity and negotiations
Policy:	Authoritarian	Liberal
Public response:	Alienation	Approval
Long-term prospects:	Concessions	Repressions

As we see, in each case political normalisation developed
according to different rules from normalisation based on
military intervention. Its scenario was different and so was
the inner logic of the political processes which took place
after peace and order was re-established. The common
features of Gomułka's and Gierek's political normalisation
were:

a) The victorious mood of the masses who, in both cases,
felt that by their action they were able not only to trigger
a major political crisis but also to enforce far-reaching
concessions which otherwise would not have taken place.

b) The reshuffle of the party leadership marking the will of the party to carry out a policy which would find popular support.

c) The declining curve of reforms, that is, the shift of emphasis in the policy pursued by the leadership from their initial pledge to implement some far-reaching reforms to a more cautious and moderate approach based on the preservation of the Soviet-type system of administration and management.

In spite of all the differences in normalisation under Gomułka and Gierek, there was a striking similarity in the development of the situation under their respective rules. Some sociologists were even inclined to speak of the 'ritualisation' of the ways by which the party dealt with the crisis in the nineteen-seventies. However, such generalisations proved misleading; they overlooked the cumulative effect of repetitive social processes, the superimposition of new contradictions over old and the impact of past experience on collective memory and collective actions.

As we shall see, the options open to Gierek when he carried out his programme of normalisation were narrower than those available to Gomułka. The political constraints of a government based on consensus did not allow him to adopt the strategies which helped Kadar revive the economy. Kadar was able to break the resistance of his own bureaucracy in carrying out reforms which modified the character of the whole economy. None of these policies could be followed by Gierek.

One of the most peculiar features of normalisation achieved under Gierek was the inability of the new leadership to carry out any effective reforms of management. Whilst Gomułka was able to dispose of some of the most conspicuous features of the Stalinist methods of planning and tolerated, for some time at least, the Workers' Councils, Gierek's regime adopted almost from the start a conservative attitude. Poland was in that respect a world apart from Hungary where Kadar was carrying out a most advanced programme of economic reforms, thoroughly transforming the Hungarian economy and giving it a tremendous push towards market socialism.

The secret of Kadar's success is to be sought in the power structure in Hungary where the position of the leader remained unchallenged under the Russian umbrella and gave him the chance to override the vested interests of many groups opposing economic reforms (Vali, 1972).

Kadar was faced by the resistance of the party and state bureaucracies who saw their influence diminished and transferred to the enterprises. Many cuts in the central apparatus meant that former functionaries either lost their jobs or were compelled to look for employment in the provinces where enterprises were located. The local bureaucracy was also dissatisfied because its influence on industry was curtailed and economic interests acquired priority over political ones, a situation resented particularly strongly by the police and security forces. In spite of all these opponents of economic reforms, Kadar was able to break through and to achieve in a relatively short time a completely new mode of running economic affairs (see Burks, 1973, p.394).

As far as his own bureaucracy was concerned, Gierek was weaker than Kadar and from the start had to zig-zag to avoid a direct confrontation with the hard-liners within the party élite.

One could venture a hypothesis that political normalisation unlike military normalisation tended to produce a weaker leadership. On the one hand, the party leaders had to face the restive workers and proceed very slowly to try to appease the people; on the other hand, they had to cope with possible dissent within their own ranks where the middle-way policy of political normalisation was bound to be opposed by both the liberal and hawkish groups within the party élite.

Gomułka and Gierek faced the same problem of how to deal with internal opposition, but while Gomułka was able to play the liberals against the hard-liners and vice versa, Gierek led a party in which the liberal wing was almost non-existent and in the first place had to accommodate conservative pressures and sectional interests.

This imbalance contributed to what we would call the internal inconsistency of the system; on the one hand the situation demanded either radical reforms or heavy-handed measures to keep things under control, whilst on the other hand the authorities were less and less able to undertake any of the alternative ways open to them. In contrast to Gomułka, whose political position was at first relatively strong, Gierek's normalisation was from the start influenced by the discrepancy between the objectives and the political means available for implementing them.

The whole balance was based on the trade-off between the improvement in living standards and the preservation of the authoritarian rule of the party but this trade-off was backed not by the coercive force of the state but by the unstable and fragile consensus of the masses and the bureaucrats whose position was stronger than ever before. The room for manoeuvre was very limited. The party–state had lost its major advantage in managing social affairs, that is, its unlimited power *vis-à-vis* its own citizens and the sectional interests of the bureaucratic establishment, without gaining the unqualified support of the population. The alternative was either bribing the masses by immediate gratification or building up an economic strategy in which temporary restraints would be rewarded by long-term improvement of living standards and general affluence. In that respect Gomułka was in a much better position than Gierek. He was able to carry out political pledges which helped him to stabilise the system, while Gierek's pledges were purely economic and would have required an economic miracle in a situation of a destabilising price-freeze and repressed inflation.

Among the specific destabilising factors which were to contribute some time later to the dramatic downfall of the new leader, the following should be mentioned:

1) The quasi-social contract between the party and the people through which the party took full responsibility for the success of the new economic policy.

2) The increased self-confidence of the working class.

3) The increased role of the party in running state affairs with the resulting alienation of the masses and ossification of official political life.

4) The contradiction between the simmering pluralisation of

political and cultural life in Poland and the rigidity of
party–state rule.

SOCIAL CONTRACT

The concept of social contract was never popular in the
Communist political doctrine. Social contract implies obliga-
tions on the part of the authorities and rights on the part of
the citizens, that is, principles which go against the
foundations of a bureaucratic power structure. Moreover,
the party is seen as the embodiment of the interests of the
working class while social contract implies two separate
parties, the government and the population.

Yet the term itself reflected very well the specific situation
in which order was restored, not by military intervention but
by a tacit agreement between the party–state élite and the
rioting masses. The workers who grudgingly stopped their
demonstrations and strikes after Gierek conceded all their
economic demands, established in fact a new relationship
between the masses and the authorities. Gierek's pledge
expressed the wish of the party to satisfy the material
well-being of the workers in exchange for their co-operation
with the new leadership. His famous question addressed to
workers in Gdańsk: 'Will you help?'—and the workers'
answer: 'We will', had a meaning which was by no means
rhetorical; the power of the workers and the desire of the
party to have their support was publicly acknowledged.
Further concessions had the same character; the workers
were perfectly aware that the decisions about price-freezing
were enforced by their determination to continue the
strikes. They accepted the promises and declarations of the
party bosses with a marked caution and restraint which
vividly contrasted with the wild enthusiasm that accompanied Gomułka's rise to power in 1956.

The very position of the party was undermined by the
deal. For the first time the distinction between 'we' (the
workers) and 'them' (the party) was officially recognised.
While, during the summer of 1956 party members among the
workers were usually the first to voice their discontent and

gave a lead to their fellow workers in convening workers' councils, in the strikes of 1970 party members in the factories were silent and the workers came forward as a united force defying the party policies.

The terms of the trade-off between the masses and the party were also very different for Gierek's team. They implied a rapid improvement in living standards, although it was obvious from the start that the authorities could not control the economic situation totally and much of what had been said by that time reflected wishful thinking on both sides. The shops were supposed to be full, food prices were to be kept low, current wages were bound to ensure decent living standards and any delay in fulfilling these expectations was to be regarded as a sign of ill-will or blatant incompetence on the part of the government. Failure to meet the expectations of the people would in those circumstances inevitably bring the party and its leadership into complete disrepute.

In the early years of his rule, Gomułka was cautious not to make lavish promises and used to emphasise that the improvement in living standards could not go beyond what the nation could produce. He was subsequently blamed for his caution and petty-mindedness, but these accusations, when made by the new élite, contributed even further to rising popular expectations. This put additional pressure on the leadership to live up to the new standards they had promulgated since taking over from their predecessors. The party had reached a point of no return: it had committed itself to the new policy.

The workers were praised for their wisdom in opposing Gomułka's ill-fated policies, extolled for their determination in fighting for a new economic strategy and referred to as a party in the nationwide deal. At the same time they were deprived of any institutional forms in which to express their views and demands within the new establishment they had brought to life. Social contract was thus to remain a redundant concept without any direct bearing on reality; it was supposed to legitimise Gierek's rise to power without acknowledging any political rights of the workers within the institutional power structure.

THE NEW WORKING CLASS

Since 1956 the workers in Poland have become a political force with whom all governments have to reckon. Their resistance to governmental policies in 1956, 1970 and 1976 was followed by substantial concessions to their demands. Yet well documented evidence, to mention only accounts of the strikes in the USSR by Albert Boiter (1964) and Betsy Gidwitz (1982) or in Rumania by Nelson (1981), contradicts the view that only Polish workers were prepared to protest against unsatisfactory economic policy within the Soviet bloc.

Zasławsky (1982, p.52) points out that in the USSR Krushchev's decision to increase food prices led to workers' agitation and, later, to the Novocherkassk revolt and he argues:

> Though totally excluded from any decision-making and subject to extremely harsh deprivations because of forced industrialisation and terror, the Soviet citizen, beginning with Stalin, could still expect a better tomorrow. This expectation has been one of the key elements in Soviet political culture. . . . Any reductions in current living standards have produced immediate upsurges in solidarity and the possibility of collective action.

In discussing the workers' attitudes, Zasławsky and many other scholars agree that the rebellious mood is particularly strong among skilled workers when their expectations are frustrated: their overall aspirations are high; as far as consumer goods are concerned their needs are more sophisticated and therefore less easily satisfied in conditions of poor economic performance. Better educated than unskilled workers they are also more articulate in pressing their demands and defying party bosses (see Pravda, 1982).

In comparison with workers in other Communist countries, Polish workers are certainly less deferential, more confident of their own importance and more rebellious in their response to unpopular policies of the government. Their Catholicism reinforced their opposition to the stereotype of the Communist worker conveyed by the propaganda of the party–state. They believed in God, followed Catholic traditions and listened to the sermons of local priests.

In the nineteen-seventies, the number of workers was rapidly increasing as a result of accelerated industrialisation. Their educational standards were also rising: on average they were much better educated than in the previous decade. The number of young vocational school-leavers was reaching a peak. Young workers were of a different breed than their fathers. Many of them had solid urban backgrounds, were educated in good schools, developed new cultural needs and discovered the appeal of modern consumerism together with many forms of youth subculture imported from the West. They were oblivious of the ruthless rule of Stalinism in Poland in the early nineteen-fifties and did not experience the economic deprivations so characteristic of those times. Brought up in the years of relative liberalism of Gomułka's regime and maturing in the years of the early boom of the nineteen-seventies, they displayed expectations and aspirations typical of consumer societies.

The economic situation made it easy for them to get the jobs they wanted and to earn enough money to satisfy their needs. Many of them were able to travel abroad, some managed to work there, earn foreign currency and buy fashionable consumer goods produced in the West. Their needs were shaped by the patterns conveyed by Western films, Western advertisements and massive quantities of goods imported from abroad. Their assessment of the economic situation in Poland was no longer based on comparisons between the deprivations of the countryside and the relative affluence of the city dwellers. They compared their living standards with those of the workers in the West and were quick to notice the relevant differences in the level of payments, range of consumer goods available in the market and housing standards. They proved to be much more critical towards the authorities than other workers in Eastern Europe and much more prone to blame the party for all the economic difficulties they experienced.

In 1976 when the workers resisted the authorities' new attempt to raise prices, the government did not hold out. The proposed price increases were promptly withdrawn in spite of an initial display of force on the part of the government. The riots were brutally suppressed but the government did not persist in their repressive policies. After a short period of ostensible retaliation the workers accused of vandalism and hooliganism were released, although they were never rehabilitated. The government adopted a policy of bribing the most important sections of the working class by securing special deliveries of high-quality food to selected factories and important industrial centres. At the same time, new methods of dealing with restive workers were developed. The authorities tried to single out those workers who were branded as troublemakers. They were sacked from more lucrative jobs, pestered by the police and often sent to jail accused of petty offences which were simple fabrications or which would otherwise be tolerated. Cases of brutal treatment of detained workers were numerous. The workers also felt more and more alienated from the factory management who ruled the factories in an authoritarian way. However, at the same time, all workers' demands backed up by short strikes or threats of such strikes, were dealt with positively and promptly by the management.

To summarise: political normalisation implemented by Gierek did not help to ease the tension between the party–state bureaucracy and the working class. On the contrary, the workers became more independent and self-confident. At the same time, they became more rebellious and embittered in view of the government's policy which not only failed to deliver the goods but also manifested the party's determination to prevent the workers from speaking their minds.

THE PARTY–STATE APPARATUS

The police apparatus which was developed under the patronage of General Moczar, as part of his power struggle against Gomułka, remained intact under Gierek although its activities were closely supervised and kept within tight limits. While the early years of Gomułka's reign were marked by massive redundancies in the political police,

Gierek limited himself to a reshuffle at the top in order to retain control of the police apparatus without cutting its numbers.

The political police were never allowed to play an independent role as they did in the last years of Gomułka's rule. Gierek was well aware of the contribution of the political police to the downfall of his predecessor and was anxious to keep them under close surveillance. They were to follow strict instructions, and their functions were strictly defined and closely monitored by Stanisław Kania, Gierek's ally.

The supervision carried out by the internal security system was confined to a number of activists of the 1968 movement who were in many cases barred from employment and whose political activities were watched continuously. Their correspondence was vetted, exit visas were refused to most of them and their friends had their names recorded by the police. In many cases they were subjected to direct harassment. In the same category were some of the 'Zionists' previously singled out by the partisan faction and used as scapegoats whenever references were to be made to the internal enemy (see Hirszowicz and Szafar, 1977a and b).

Gierek's rival, Moczar, was gradually distanced from the political scene. As early as 1971 he was nominated Chairman of the Supreme Chamber of Control, a position regarded as a political dead end.

Kept under close control as far as their political functions were concerned, the members of the police force enjoyed an almost unlimited power in dealing with the public in non-political matters. The brutality of the militia had reached a hitherto unknown level. People detained for petty offences were, in many cases, severely beaten as, all too often, were those who tried to argue verbally with the militia. From 1968 when they were used on a massive scale against students demonstrating in the streets, the members of the police had acquired a feeling of power and impunity.

The general hatred for the militia found its expression in innumerable jokes about their stupidity. Many of these jokes were direct translations from English and were originally jokes about Irishmen in England and Poles in the USA. Also in circulation were many stories about police corruption and their avidity in extorting bribes from people apprehended by them. Thus, hatred and contempt went together, contributing to some extent to the alienation of the police, many of whom responded with undisguised hostility towards members of the public.

However, as far as the judicial system was concerned, the police tried to uphold an appearance of maintaining the rule of law. Following Gierek's instructions, political offenders were treated by the courts much more leniently than under Gomułka. Gierek boasted that there were virtually no political prisoners under his rule, and, indeed, this was so. When necessary, political opponents were apprehended and brought to court under fabricated accusations of disorderly behaviour or other petty offences. The court procedures were open to the public although different restrictions were imposed on the numbers attending the trials and some ugly scenes occasionally took place in the court rooms.

On the whole, however, the coercive apparatus remained in the background, powerful enough to strike when necessary but, with few exceptions, prevented from acting as an independent body.

As far as the administrative and party hierarchies were concerned, Gierek did his best to build up his own following. According to the figures presented by Błazynski, by 1971 he had replaced about 40 per cent of the district and local party leaders and by 1972 fourteen out of 18 provincial party secretaries. Of the 115 full members of the Central Committee who were elected in December 1971, only forty-nine had been members of the previous body (Blazynski, 1979, pp.88-9), but these changes were still strongly influenced by the partisan faction.

Centralisation of political command was at first regarded as a way of improving the lines of direct communication between the leadership and the workers. In June 1971 the Central Committee took over direct control of 164 party organisations in the largest Polish enterprises (Bielasiak, 1983). Visits to industrial centres by Gierek and his team, and meetings with the workers in the factories were supposed to break the rigid chain of command and communication and establish a new direct relationship between the Party Secretary and the masses.

At the same time, however, institutional reforms carried out by Gierek had the opposite effect and contributed to further alienation of the workers and the public in general. Centralisation of power at the top severed the links between the party élite and society. The remaining representative bodies gradually became redundant, the channels through which independent opinion could be voiced were blocked or silenced and the elements of pluralism based on the division of labour between party and state organs were gradually eliminated. When the Ministry of Labour, Wages and Social Affairs was created in 1972, its very existence undermined the role of trade unions on the shopfloor (Bielasiak, 1983). The strengthening of the party's position *vis-à-vis* state organs manifested itself in the decision that the secretaries of party committees in ministries and central offices were to be nominated by the Secretariat of the Central Committee. The position of these nominees was strengthened by elevating them to the status of deputy ministers (Rakowski, 1981a, p.129).

The major purge with effects favourable to Gierek's interests came with the reorganisation of local administration between 1973 and 1975, as a result of which 68,000 party officials became redundant (Blazynski, 1979, p.90), while at the same time people loyal to the new élite were flocking in.

One of the major results of the reform was to impose the party secretaries, ex officio, as heads of locally elected councils, a system which had already been in existence in Rumania since 1967 in line with the authoritarian structure of party–state rule there (Hayward and Barki, 1979).

A good summary of these reforms has been presented by Karpiński whose well documented conclusion is that they defied liberal principles and brought an overall strengthening of party–state power (Karpiński, 1982, pp.167–70).

There is no doubt that the purges and promotions reinforced Gierek's personal power but they also contributed to the weakening of the party as a whole. The old network of activists was to some extent undermined or in some cases even destroyed; the know-how of the old *apparatchiki* was discarded as not essential. The channels of informal contacts and influence among party élites on the local level had ceased to exist following the changes in administrative boundaries and the reshuffle of the party bureaucrats who were dominant in the old provinces and regions.

As we see, political normalisation did not contribute to any devolution of political power as was characteristic of the early period of Gomułka's rule. On the contrary, it brought about a powerful build-up of the centralised power structure based on the latent strength of the police and widened the gap between the party and society.

THE NEW ETHOS OF THE PARTY BUREAUCRACY

The circumstances in which Gierek built up his following differed greatly from those in which Gomułka established his leadership and resulted in the development of a new ethos of the party–state bureaucracy. Faced by the influential and well entrenched party apparatus inherited from Gomułka's time and strengthened in the fight he led against Gomułka in the late nineteen-sixties, Gierek tried to bring as many people from the provinces of Katowice and Poznań as he could. They flocked in, bringing with them the new values and ideology of parochial *arrivistes* lacking wider political experience and indifferent to the fundamentalist outlook of the Communists of the older generation in the central party apparatus. Their life experience was confined to the provincial affairs of post-war Poland; their political careers focused on personal intrigues and backstage manoeuvres. Their ideals and values centred on the possession of material goods and on consumption. Good flats and houses, expensive furniture and trips abroad were the highest targets in their careers and most convincing status symbols. Brought up in times of rising, but unfulfilled, expectations, they believed in Gierek because he was the one who promised a better life to party and state officials and openly challenged the puritan attitude of Gomułka.

Their concern for the material standards of life, stability and professional advancement was reinforced and legitimised by the political objectives set up by Gierek for the nation. Building up a consumer society matched their own aspirations and justified their greed in utilising all the advantages which the system could offer.

Their advancement constituted some sort of managerial revolution; influence shifted from the old-style party politicians towards administrators and managers within both the party and the state apparatus. Degrees in engineering were regarded as the best recommendation for administrative jobs. The urge to modernise, and admiration for advanced Western technology were part of the ideological package of the new generation of bureaucrats from whom Gierek recruited his followers. Pragmatism and technocratic philosophy were the ultimate values and were often combined with an openly cynical attitude towards the ideological heritage of Marxist socialism regarded by many as an obsolete relic of the past.

In Hungary and Czechoslovakia, where the leaders had to rationalise many unpopular policies and societies were highly polarised with regard to past experience, the party retained many characteristics of the 'élitist party'. Nothing similar occurred in Poland where the party activists could genuinely believe that in pursuing their own careers and ambitions they also expressed and carried out the aspiration of consumerism shared by the whole nation. There was no doubt that the objectives put forward by the party were popular. They were defined not in abstract ideological terms of building socialism, but referred to economic growth and improving living standards. The policy of *détente* and economic co-operation with the West justified the abandonment of Marxist language and legitimised the pragmatic arguments which served among others to bridge the ideological gap between Poland and her Western allies.

The party, as it operated under Gierek, was therefore an organisation defending the establishment, standing firmly behind the new policy and appealing to the commonsense values of self-interest, national unity and economic well-being.

The 'revisionists' and would-be reformists were already purged or effectively silenced. The only serious opponents of the new leadership were the disgruntled supporters of Moczar within the party, but they were gradually eliminated from positions of influence and regarded Gierek as a traitor who had betrayed the holy alliance of the 1968–70 movement against Gomułka. Frustrated and embittered, the Moczarites did not pose any direct threat to Gierek's policy however and, in fact, they even helped the new leader by continuing their campaign against all revisionist deviations, spotting Jews wherever they could and denouncing their nefarious ideological influence in the dissident movements.

There is no doubt that such a party offered no chance of venting or defusing social discontent when the economic situation deteriorated. There were no people within the party who would be able to oppose Gierek effectively and demand substantial reforms. Paradoxically, the only ones who expressed some arguments in favour of liberalisation and raised the merits of more democratic government in the late nineteen-seventies were Werblan and Olszowski, two ambitious politicians compromised during the anti-Semitic and anti-liberal campaign of 1968. They were frustrated by Gierek's personal policy which undermined their influence and hoped for a come-back under liberal slogans which they used to oppose and denounce the leader.

Party control over society had reached its peak. Gierek's quest for power was based on reinforcing the influence of the party apparatus to an extent that had never been achieved under Gomułka. He had played on the differences and conflicts between party and state officials, while Gierek on the other hand did his best to integrate the party–state under the party leadership.

This meant that for the man in the street the party, and the party alone, was responsible for all aspects of social life, a conviction which rebounded against the party at a time when the crisis was gathering momentum and the hour of truth was approaching.

1976—THE WRITING ON THE WALL

The food riots in 1976 marked a turning-point in the internal policy of Gierek's regime. Unable to resist massive pressure from the workers to keep food prices frozen, the government was faced with an impossible situation: aspirations and expectations were high while the ailing economy was less and less able to deliver the goods. The peace the government bought by abandoning reforms was short-lived and the so-called New Economic Manoeuvre announced as a response to the 1976 riots was nothing but a collection of patchy measures aimed at closing the most catastrophic gaps without dealing with the causes of economic imbalance.

Faced with the riots, the government decided to continue a policy which could not and would not work. It was living on borrowed time, recklessly increasing the amount of debts weighing down the economy and mortgaging the future for many years to come.

Seen from this perspective the years 1976–80 constituted the most serious indictment of the system and those representing it. The power of the party–state allowed for the continuation of a policy which was bound to end in disaster; the centralised and irresponsible character of management made things even worse than they would otherwise have been. In addition, the narrow-mindedness and self-centredness of the leadership helped to perpetuate the deadlock in which the nation was caught. The major factors in worsening the situation were: (a) control of information which prevented the population, including party activists, from gaining information about the real economic situation of the country; (b) the further ossification of the political system which eliminated any chance of effective opposition within the establishment and pushed people towards activities which made direct confrontation almost unavoidable.

Why were no attempts made to make a clean breast of it and to fully inform the nation, thereby asking for help and support? Rakowski, who comments on the behaviour of the leadership in the years after 1976, argues that they were scared. They were afraid to present an honest diagnosis of the situation because to do so would mean encouraging society to question the competence of the ruling élite to lead the country. Rakowski states: 'The authorities do not like to confess their mistakes and if they must they rectify them without anybody knowing about it.' (Rakowski, 1981a, p.45) However, these tactics were not possible after 1976 when the deterioration of the economic situation was obvious and the erratic measures undertaken as a remedy did not help in the least.

The policy after 1976 was that of zig-zagging from attempts to contain discontent by resorting to harsh measures, to steps which aimed to please the public and reinforce the image of a liberal regime resisting the pressure of hard-liners to resort to neo-Stalinist coercion. The net effect of this zig-zagging was, however, counterproductive because the government was neither feared nor liked.

THE NEW ROLE OF THE CATHOLIC CHURCH

The statement issued in the New Year of 1971 by the Chief Council of the Polish Episcopate, and read in churches, formulated the following six demands:

1 The right to freedom of conscience and freedom of religious life together with full normalisation of relations between the Church and the state.
2 The right to freely shape the culture of one's own nation, according to the spirit of the Christian principles of coexistence of people.
3 The right to social justice expressed in fulfilling just demands.
4 The right to truth in social life, to information according with the truth, and to free expression of one's views and demands.
5 The right to material conditions which ensure decent existence of the family, and of each individual citizen.
6 The right to such an attitude toward the citizens that they are not insulted, harmed and persecuted in anything.
(Radio Free Europe Research, East Europe, Poland 1, 5 January 1971, p.4).

Addressed to a population which was about 90 per cent Catholic, such a message had enormous influence and marked the determination of the Church to exert its power in shaping political life.

The Church, with its 20,000 priests, 21,000 classes organised for religious instruction of school children, forty-six seminaries training future priests and two schools of higher education, represented a powerful organisation able to exercise its spiritual rule over tens of millions of Poles (Nowak, 1982, and Zdaniewicz, 1979).

The political involvement of the Church was significant throughout the whole decade of Gierek's rule and marked a new balance of forces within a Communist society.

Under the leadership of Cardinal Stefan Wyszyński, a powerful personality, the Church took a stand in all important political debates including, in January 1976, the open protest against the amendments of the Polish Constitution. The Church constituted a most effective umbrella for political dissent. After 1968 many persecuted intellectuals including Jews found a platform in Catholic journals and magazines, and students expelled from the state universities were able to continue their studies at the Catholic university of Lublin.

In the late nineteen-seventies, when political opposition was gathering momentum, the support of the Church became most important. Authors whose writings were banned by state-controlled publishing houses and journalists who were barred from employment in the state-controlled Press, were able to publish in Catholic magazines, some of them using pen-names (because of formal censorship restrictions) but these pseudonyms were known to everybody. Clubs for the Catholic intelligentsia were centres for free political discussions and after 1976 many young members of the clubs co-operated with the Workers' Defence Committee (KOR) and rebellious students' committees. The Church was always taking a firm stand against the violation of human rights by the authorities and supported the victims of political persecutions. After the repressions of 1976 against the workers, the Church protested against harsh punishments and later demanded amnesty for the imprisoned workers. Church support for cultural freedom was also very strong. In response to campaigns against the Flying University, the Bishops' Conference on 9 March 1978 stated: 'The restriction of science and research together with artistic and religious activity through censorship is regrettable . . . because the nation has a right to know the objective truth about itself.' (Polish SR/7, RFER, 27 March 1978, item 1.)

In Cracow, Wojtyła offered rooms to the Flying University lecturers which guaranteed them and their students safety.

In spite of severe censorship restrictions on Catholic publications (see, *Czarna Księga Cenzury PRL*, 1978 and 1979), the voice of the Church could reach the majority of the Polish population by reading out letters from the Church authorities in the churches. Important sermons of Cardinal Wyszyński were widely reported in foreign broadcasts in Polish. The weaker the ideological message of the party, the more powerful was the voice of the Church in expressing the demands of the majority.

In the face of growing discontent, Gierek found it necessary to look for support from Cardinal Wyszyński. To achieve this aim he took steps towards establishing co-operation between the state and Church authorities. He could rightly expect the Cardinal to help him.

The first official meeting between Gierek and Wyszyński took place on 29 October 1977. A few weeks later Gierek was received by Pope Paul VI and a series of visits by Cardinal Casaroli to Poland brought forward negotiations which later led to the invitation of the Polish Pope to Warsaw.

Although the Church tried to maintain the balance between its religious functions and its role as the representative of the nation and dissociate itself from direct involvement in political opposition, many individual priests and lay activists of the Catholic intelligentsia joined the dissidents. Priest Zieja was a prominent member of KOR (Lipski, 1983, p.51). Many others actively supported the opposition or participated in the activities of the independent cultural associations and clubs.

One of the most interesting phenomena was the development of the youth movement 'Light and Life' under the guidance of the priest Franciszek Błachnicki. The movement grew out of the tradition of Catholic youth festivals and summer youth camps but its characteristic feature was a high level of centralised organisation, a massive membership and an active involvement in current political issues (RFE Research, Poland, 24 June 1980).

In comparison with the bureaucratised and faceless youth organisations sponsored by the party, the 'Light and Life' movement represented a genuine grass roots organisation based on thousands of activists and responding to the needs of youth for recreation, music, summer camps, religious ceremonies and active involvement in the most important political and cultural issues. The founder of the movement, Priest Błachnicki, belonged to the most outspoken critics of the government among the Polish clergy. He presented the movement activists with an alternative ideology based on religion but taking a firm stand about the evils of political life.

He interpreted evangelism as being closely connected with the idea of the liberation of man, he attacked school textbooks for the lies they contained, praised the courage and solidarity of the opposition movement and preached the unity of faith and active participation in social and political life to implement religious ideals.

The Church did not seem to approve in full the bypassing of the existing hierarchy and Church institutions by the movement, and was reluctant to encourage direct political involvement of members of the movement, but there were many rank-and-file priests who fully identified with Błachnicki's teachings. A complicated system of gradual initiation in the ideals of the movement reinforced its appeal and allowed a hard core of dedicated members to become established.

The election of Karol Wojtyła to the Papacy became the major event in establishing the new role of the Church in Poland. The authority of the Pope counterbalanced the role of the party–state establishment and became a symbol of national unity. The Church publicly claimed its position as spiritual leader of the nation as a whole. The overwhelming majority of the population supported this claim and were united in public commitment to the newly elected Polish Pope.

Gierek's decision to allow the papal visit was certainly a

big gamble in his desperate search for powerful allies in the years of growing discontent. The visit was regarded by many observers as a turning-point in the relationships between the party and society. The organisation of the ceremonies and maintenance of law and order was left entirely to the Church—a fact which in itself was unprecedented and gave the Church the chance to develop a nationwide organisation of Church wardens directing and supervising the enormous crowds participating in religious celebrations and meetings with the Pope. Suddenly the state, with its enormous apparatus of power, was presented as redundant, while millions of Catholics were participating in a nationwide exercise of self-organisation and self-discipline.

The symbolic impact of the visit was enormous; religious feelings reached their height and the public influence of the Church instantly became a most important component of national life. Although the spiritual role of the Church was in itself nothing new, for the first time since 1945 the right of Catholics to self-organisation was publicly acknowledged and reinforced in the minds of the millions who participated in the celebrations (Lipski, 1983, p.285-91).

Thus, although the short-term effect of the papal visit could have been regarded by Gierek as a stabilising factor, in the long run the visit became one of the major forces undermining the claim of the government to absolute rule over the nation.

NEW ASPECTS OF POLITICAL OPPOSITION

The opposition movement in Poland was by no means an isolated phenomenon. There is no doubt that the Conference on Security and Co-operation in Europe which took place in Helsinki between 3 July and 1 August 1975, had a tremendous influence on the whole dissident movement in Eastern Europe including the USSR:

In October 1975 Andrei Sacharov was awarded a Nobel prize.

In Czechoslovakia a thousand signatories came forward with their Charter of Human Rights.

In Rumania in February 1977 the Goma group directed an appeal to the Helsinki signatories.

In Hungary *samizdat* publications were mushrooming.

In Yugoslavia the left-wing Praxis group and two groups of Serbian and Croatian nationalists were active.

In East Germany protests followed the stripping of his nationality from Wolf Bierman, a well known song writer, who was forbidden to come back after a concert tour in West Germany.

The follow-up meeting in Belgrade two years after the Helsinki conference reinforced the general pressure for democratic change and respect for civil rights by the Communist governments.

In Poland the opposition movement developed later than in the USSR (see Matejko, 1980). The movement was activated by the events of 1976 when, after years of relative isolation, the dissident intellectuals found themselves in the forefront of the fight in support of the workers (Raina, 1978, Lipski, 1983). Many aspects of the movement were certainly similar to those in other Communist countries but its sympathy with the grievances of persecuted workers from the start gave the opposition new scope for its activities.

In all Communist countries of Eastern Europe, the intervention in Czechoslovakia marked an abrupt end to the reformist hope that Communist parties might be transformed from within and elaborate an alternative to the Soviet model of government. For all practical purposes, revisionism was dead (see Kusin, 1976 and 1978), and the political opposition looked for support not among the party liberals but from the public at large (Connor, 1980). This situation removed important ideological restraints which held back the reformist trend before 1968. The dissidents did not care about the doctrinal acceptability of their views to the forces of the establishment (Rupnik, 1979), did not hesitate to seek support and co-operation with the Church and looked for their ideological roots in the non-Communist traditions of pre-war Poland. While, a few years earlier, two leading Polish 'dissidents', Kuroń and Modzelewski, had presented views close to those of the radical Marxist heritage (Kuroń and Modzelewski, 1969), they became gradually more and more inclined to look for inspiration to, and to base their criticism on the teachings of social-democratic thinkers (Kuroń, 1977). The early activists of the opposition represented a broad front of liberal and democratic groups while many dissidents later extended their search for ideological roots to the writings of Józef Piłsudski and Roman Dmowski whose programmes and policies dominated pre-war Poland.

It should be noted that the policy of *détente* created a new chance for the dissidents to co-operate with enlightened public opinion in the West, to utilise the support of the Polish diaspora in the West and to benefit from the free flow of ideas between West and East.

In spite of all similarities with other dissident movements in Eastern Europe, the opposition in Poland operated from the start in specific circumstances which were determined by (a) the crisis of 1976 which created their alliance with the workers; (b) the critical situation of the Polish leadership in view of the approaching economic crisis; and (c) the new balance of political forces established after 1976.

The emergence of open organised dissent was preceded by the wave of protests connected with the amendment of the Polish constitution. This was the first genuine political campaign since 1968, initiated from below and not orchestrated by the party (see: 'The Letter of 59 Intellectuals,' 1976, and Lipski, 1983, pp.24-5).

Faced by growing economic and political difficulties, Gierek was inclined to support the doctrine of integration under Soviet leadership in a much more comprehensive way than some other members of the Communist bloc. Constitutional changes were part of the package.

Under the umbrella of legitimate discussion about the proposed changes to the constitution, massive campaigns against new versions of the constitution developed. A wide wave of protests was fuelled by the unpopular changes introduced in the new version of the constitution which included a strong emphasis on the role of the USSR and a direct reference to the leading role of the party following the example of other East European constitutions and, above all, of the USSR.

A new and decisive impulse for the development of political opposition was generated by the ruthless measures taken against the workers who participated in the 1976 riots. It was then that the Workers' Defence Committee (KOR) was created (see Lipski, 1983), an unprecedented development in Poland which turned dissent into political action, going further than the Soviet dissident groups—such as the Initiative Group, the Human Rights Committee, Group 73 and the Helsinki Watch Group—that had emerged earlier.

In contrast to all these groups which in the USSR were pursuing wider political objectives, KOR started with the very specific purpose of acting on behalf of the workers and this had from the start a wide appeal for the public and the workers in particular. The widespread repressions and hatred of the militia among workers and peasants who were the most likely to fall victim to police brutality for petty offences, contributed to the popularity of KOR's objectives long after the original cause for its convention ceased to exist (see Lipski, 1983).

The emergence of KOR undoubtedly marked a new period in the political history of Poland and the fact that in spite of police harassment and the frequent temporary apprehensions of its members KOR survived and was able to develop its activities without its members being tried and sentenced, had a snowball effect on the development of political opposition in Poland (Raina, 1981).

In March 1977, a new group, ROPCiO, emerged bringing new political overtones of nationalist traditions devoid of any references to socialism. A year later there were already several different groups and committees with their own programmes and activities ranging from public debates to editing magazines and organising public demonstrations.

In succeeding years KOR retained its leading position in the opposition movement in spite of the limited number of its members. The respect it enjoyed, the moral integrity of its activists and the intellectual calibre of the leading group accounted for the charismatic leadership of this group in the Polish opposition movement of the late nineteen-seventies.

The most important aspect of the activities of the Polish dissidents, apart from the legal defence and support of the workers carried out by KOR, was the publishing of books and magazines. This action went far beyond the classic *samizdat*, a form of transmitting written texts in the USSR. KOR was able to publish not only journals, of which *Robotnik*, *Zapis* and *Krytyka* were the most important, but also several brochures and books based on advanced printing techniques (Kryński, 1978). In 1977 the Independent Publishing House, NOWA, was created which in the first few years published several dozen books.

Other 'dissident' groups followed the same pattern. In April 1977, ROPCiO started publishing the journal *Opinia* and, later, several new titles appeared, some of them produced by small splinter groups with literary or political ambitions, to present an independent forum for uncensored poems, novels, reportage or literary essays. Moreover, uncensored publications included reprints of most popular books from before the war, including Piłsudski's works, Roman Dmowski's essays, etc.

In dealing with the opposition, Gierek was restrained not merely by the spirit and letter of the Helsinki agreements which on the surface at least he tried to respect, but also by the general objectives of his policy which implied maintaining wide contacts with the West, allowing people to travel abroad and leaving a wide margin in the economy for the private sector (see Summerscale, 1982, p.41).

Table 6·1 Travel from and to Poland

	1977	1978	1979
Poles travelling abroad			
To: Eastern bloc countries	11,894,000	10,602,000	8,800,000
Western countries	518,000	539,000	635,000
Foreigners travelling to Poland			
From: Eastern bloc countries	9,611,000	9,712,000	8,100,000
Western countries	934,000	983,000	1,018,000

(RFE, Research Report, p.12, Poland/12, 11 June, Item 4.)

The open-door policy adopted by Gierek gave Poles incomparably more chance to maintain contacts with the' West than any other East European nation. While some prominent dissidents and their sympathisers were refused exit visas for travelling abroad, many others were free to travel as they wished. The access of foreign correspondents to Poland was also unrestricted and their visits reached an unprecedented level so that all political events in Poland could easily be monitored. All facts regarding abuses of the law and political persecutions were widely publicised by Western mass media, and telephone hot-lines immediately supplied information of interest to public opinion in the West. Articles by leading dissidents were published in the Western press and by the Polish publishing houses in the West like Kultura or Aneks. Most of these publications were easily obtainable in Poland from people travelling abroad: the best known of these were the publications of the Literary Institute in Paris, and Aneks. Western broadcasts in Polish were partly jammed although BBC programmes in Polish were usually tolerated. The wide use of tape-recorders permitted the reproduction of many important messages.

Economic sanctions against members of the opposition also became less effective. Some could rely on financial help or fees from publications coming from abroad. The younger members were able to carry out odd jobs allowing them to make a living without being formally employed in the public sector and exposed to the economic harassment of the authorities.

The government's attempts to introduce a law against parasites which could be used as a weapon against the dissidents failed to materialise in view of the resistance of legal and intellectual circles.

The authorities obviously preferred some sort of containment policy aimed at isolating opposition to arrests and harsh prison sentences. The opposition was harassed, their criticism was dismissed as allegedly based on ill-will and subversive intentions. Critics of the system were presented to the public as enemies of socialism whose main or even unique objective was to serve the interests of Western imperialism. As usual, in many articles these accusations were associated with hints about the Jewish origin of some of the leading dissidents so as to substantiate the view that they were serving international Zionism and acting out of hatred towards the Polish nation (Hirszowicz and Szafar, 1977a and b).

The authorities possessed a wide range of instruments of political and administrative retributions and harassment. Jan Jozef Lipski in his *KOR* enumerates the following: dismissals from jobs, the blocking of promotions and transfers to other jobs; relegation of rebellious students and children of dissidents from the universities and other schools of higher education; instructions for censors to stop all publications by the dissidents and eliminate all references to their cultural and professional activities; surveillance, interrogations and detentions for short periods; temporary arrests; house searches; kidnapping; severe beatings (ending sometimes with the death of the victims); planting listening devices; pestering with abusive telephone calls; public slanders; fabricating documents and rumours by which false accusations were supposedly corroborated; threats of death and injury; destruction of personal property; inscription of doors; and anti-Semitic campaigns (Lipski, 1983, p.109–23).

This long list did not include other reprisals which were the favourite weapon of the Soviet authorities: exile to remote areas of the country; eviction from towns of residence; incarceration in mental asylums; and exile abroad.

FACADE AND REALITIES OF POLITICAL LIFE

The outbreak of political and cultural activities outside the establishment contrasted with the growing ossification of party–state rule which displayed more and more symptoms of bureaucratic decay. There was an inverse relationship between the growing tendency of Gierek's team to control all aspects of inner party and state activities on the official level and their inability to cope with and contain the growing restiveness of the population in all its informal expressions. Successive centralising reforms of mass organisations, associations and local councils contributed to this development. The growing control of the mass media remained also in striking contrast with the massive increase of unofficial and uncensored publications.

In 1957 Professor Hochfeld, a member of the Polish Diet, asserted:

Today as in the past the struggle for democratic rights and freedoms is accompanied by, and culminates in, the emergence of various types of voluntary associations and organisations, thanks to which society ceases to be 'atomised' in the face of the power of the state and becomes 'articulated'. Particular classes, strata and social groups impart a distinctive character to these associations and organisations and leave their imprint on the rights and freedoms won as a result of their struggle. If one speaks of an institutional guarantee of civil rights and freedoms, then the emergence and functioning of such institutions as local self-government, trade unions, economic associations, scientific organisations, etc., play an extraordinarily important role . . . . [On the other hand] it is a characteristic phenomenon that the liquidation or absorption by the state of all public associations—of all the traditional forms through which particular classes, strata and social groups are 'articulated'—as a rule accompanies every policy of eliminating democratic rights and freedoms, [every] dictatorial, totalistic policy. (Quoted by Terry, in Simon and Kanet, 1981, p.31).

The policy pursued by Gierek incorporated all those principles which were enumerated by Hochfeld as measures associated with the elimination of democratic rights and freedoms. W. Pańków characterised Gierek's policy as an attempt to reintroduce the 'pure' socialist model, somewhat sullied in the period of 'errors and distortions' the events in October 1956. He enumerated the following measures as most symptomatic of this tendency:

(1) Fusion of youth organisations and their subordination to a single controlling centre, and thereby to the Polish United Workers' Party, which put an end to the traditional, though very limited, autonomy of the pathfinders', students' and young peasants' organisations.
(2) fusion of co-operatives and their subordination to a single controlling centre with a single system of swelled administration, which in practice amounted to the nationalisation of co-operatives.
(3) subordination of small-scale production to the central authorities, which practically annihilated that sphere of the national economy.
(4) putting an end to the market connections (revived for a short time) between town and country, between agriculture and the rest of the national economy, through the subordination of agriculture and the rural areas in general to the reformed local administration, in particular to the head officers of the communes. . .

(5) subordination of economic (and other) organisations both to the central administrative apparatus . . . and the executive bodies of the Polish United Workers' Party. . .
(6) growing subordination of culture, education, university schools and research institutions to the State administration, on the one hand, and to the PUWP apparatus on the other.
(7) silencing by the State as the promoter of cultural activity of those authors and artists whose work did not comply with the standards set by representatives of the PUWP apparatus. (Pańków, 1982, p.41-2).

The growth of the administrative apparatus was an inevitable outcome of such policies. And this growth stimulated in turn further attempts at extending the control of the state over society.

The following table, prepared by Mieczyslaw Rakowski, illustrates the growing centralisation of administration:

Table 6·2 Centralisation and growth of administration

	1970	1978	increase of persons	1970=100
Prime Minister	1	1	—	100
Deputy prime ministers	7	9	2	128.6
Deputy heads of Planning Commission	6	11	5	193.3
Ministers (members of government)	23	32	9	139.1
Heads of committees	3	—	−3	—
Heads of central offices	22	18	−4	81.8
Vice-ministers	80	137	57	171.2
Minister Wieczorek	1	1	—	—
Under-secretaries of the office of the Council of Ministers	—	3	3	—
TOTALS	143	212	69	148.3

Source: Rakowski (1980).

The process of liquidation or absorption by the state of all organisations in which independent views could be voiced developed with enormous speed in the years of the growing crisis. Gierek was anxious to suppress all signs of dissent within the ranks of his own bureaucracy, to eradicate all articulation of independent views in state-controlled organisations and to strangle all institutions by direct control of the party *apparatchiki*. As in the early years of Stalinist policy, this process prevented possible rebellion in the ranks of party activists and state bureaucrats and among the party-dominated intelligentsia.

Contrary to Stalinist practice this policy was, however, not associated with the stifling of public opinion and suppression of independent institutions beyond the realm of the party–state, hence the paradox we have mentioned: the less articulated was the dissent within the official structures, the stronger it resounded outside them.

Reform of the students' organisation started a series of party struggles and ended in the total submission of the students to the political control of the party. At the same time, this very policy triggered students' protests which did not calm down but gradually grew into open dissent with increased numbers of students joining the network of KOR sympathisers and building up independent students' bodies.

Amendments to the constitution, although watered down under pressure of public opinion, did not succeed in preventing rapid growth of anti-Soviet feelings and decline of the authority of the party whose leading role was to be confirmed by the constitution.

The administrative reforms of 1972–5 strengthened Gierek's influence among party and state officials at the local level but contributed to the alienation of the population deprived of the few rights they enjoyed in their dealings with local councils and faced by the despotic rule of local party secretaries.

The deterioration of relations between government and peasants was another effect of a neo-Stalinist policy aimed at increasing administrative control of the central authorities over the agricultural sector.

There is no doubt that the dissatisfaction of the peasantry with the agricultural policy of the government was growing. In an opinion poll carried out in November/December 1980, it was revealed that more peasants regarded the policy in the late nineteen-seventies as more harmful to their interests than the policy under Stalin. The following, expressed in percentages, are the answers to the question: At what time was the policy of the state least beneficial for agriculture?

Table 6·3 Answers indicating years of least beneficial policy of the
state for agriculture

1944–48	8.0
1949–55	27.9
1956–63	1.5
1964–70	3.5
1971–75	1.5
1976–80	39.4
Other answers	4.0
Don't knows	14.1

Source: Dziatłowicki (1981).

It was, however, in the administration of the mass media
that Gierek's victory–defeat syndrome was most spectacular. The information gap in Poland was probably less
pronounced than in any other East European country.
Nevertheless, the expectations of the people were aroused
and the discrepancy between the official version of what was
going on in the economy and the realities of everyday life
deprived the mass media of much of their credibility. The
first attempts to maintain the bonds with the masses were
short-lived: the so-called Citizens' Tribune on television was
abandoned, press conferences became less and less frequent
and information about the activities of the Political Bureau
and Central Committee was minimal.

The struggle for complete conformity of party-controlled
newspapers was almost totally won: a combination of tough
censorship, personnel purges and ruthless punishments of
insubordinate journalists allowed Gierek to almost eradicate
any signs of dissent in public life. The central and most
influential institution, the Broadcasting and Television
Affairs Committee, was dictatorially managed by one of
Gierek's staunchest supporters, Maciej Szczepański.

At no time in Polish post-war history, and in no other
Communist country, has underground uncensored literature
been so widely issued and so popular among its readers.
Dozens of new titles by dissident groups appeared each year
and an independent publishing house came into being which
produced several volumes which were banned by official
publishing boards. The prohibited studies which appeared

abroad and were not accessible to the majority of Poles were also reprinted and distributed almost openly under the eyes of the police.

Data relating to the decaying economy which were banned by censors from official news were quoted in much detail by uncensored leaflets, and unorthodox comments explained the real meaning of economic difficulties. A spectacular development was the smuggling out of the whole rule-book of the censors; the book was published abroad, smuggled into Poland and hundreds of copies were distributed (*Czarna Księga Cenzury*). The duller the official newspapers, the more interested were people in unofficial publications and the greater was the influence of uncensored studies.

This dualism appeared not only in mass media but in all other spheres of public life, where ritualistic behaviour developed out of all proportion. Gierek, whilst visiting the mines, was photographed with happily smiling miners, and delivered speeches at official conferences. He was applauded at state-sponsored festivities and festivals while at the same time the country was displaying a more and more rebellious mood.

The gap between the façade and reality developed even within the bureaucratic apparatus. The tendencies of centralisation had developed on an enormous scale but at the same time the party leadership yielded to powerful lobbies which frustrated all attempts to carry out a consistent economic and social policy. Therefore, on the surface there was an appearance of unity and discipline while, at the same time, sectional interests tore the economy apart and paralysed any efforts at effective reconstruction. As far as the lobbies were concerned, Gierek's influential adviser. Paweł Bożyk stated the following:

In the seventies the freedom of choice of the central authorities was not unlimited. Formally they could take any decisions they wanted, especially because they were subject to no control. In practice, however, tactics dominated over strategy. The decision-makers at the top were subject to the influences of omnipotent lobbies (mining, steelworks, motor-car industry and many others). Each lobby tried to find a sponsor on the highest level. The mining lobby was in the best position, although the

others also created their own high-level representatives. In fact, squab-
bling took place between different pressure groups and the result of this
struggle decided the allocation of resources. The members of the highest
leadership did not dare to fight against particular interests—they were
afraid that a lobby would destroy everybody who revealed such an
intention, irrespective of the position he occupied. In most cases the
members of different lobbies remained anonymous, apart from the deputy
prime minister, minister and one or two directors. Yet the strength of
influence of different lobbies was enormous because it reached everywhere, ruthlessly vilified its adversaries up to their total destruction . . .
without liquidating this situation there was no chance to carry out any
economic reform. (ITD, 3 July 1983, Doradcy.)

The appearance of outward discipline helped many
bureaucratic groups to pursue their own interests; they were
able to win the approval of the political leader by paying
lip-service to his views and displaying external signs of
loyalty. The weakening of internal control was one of the
specific characteristics of the system and in these circumstances the chances of manipulation and deception on the part
of different interest groups within the bureaucracy was
increasing. Corruption was part of the game since those in
control could be bribed to co-operate with the culprits.

The policy of centralisation served not so much to
improve administrative efficiency (indeed the opposite
resulted from it) but to tighten political control over the
opponents and critics of the leader and his team. Tight
control over information was his major weapon in that
respect.

The price to be paid for this secrecy was, however,
enormous. Very few people, even among the élite, were
aware of the gravity of the economic situation and were
therefore inclined to attribute all difficulties and shortcomings to the inefficiency of their leader alone. The tighter the
control of economic information in the late nineteen-
seventies, the greater was the undercurrent of criticism
directed against Gierek's team among the state and party
functionaries who experienced the deficiency of the system.
For all those who were not aware of the situation, the
greater was the shock when the facts came to light.

Contrary to much current opinion, the mood in Poland on
the eve of the new crisis was rather optimistic; people

noticed the deterioration of the economic situation but they were not aware of the gravity of the crisis and believed that the shortcomings were mainly due to the inefficiency of the ruling élite. About 60 per cent of people in Poland believed that in the next five years, i.e., 1980-5, their economic situation would improve and only 8 per cent assessed their prospects in a pessimistic way (Beskid, 1980, p.373).

THE SUPERIMPOSITION OF POLITICAL AND ECONOMIC CRISIS

The peculiar combination of the arbitrary rule of the leadership together with their impotence *vis-à-vis* society, the economy and even their own subordinate bureaucracies, contributed to the development of the political crisis. Unable to solve any problems, Gierek concentrated his efforts on maintenance of the status quo.

Faced by growing economic difficulties and the restiveness of the people, he did not expect any forgiveness or understanding from his rivals who blamed him not only for economic policy but also for his indecision in dealing with the political opposition.

As long as the economic situation in Poland was bearable, the containment policy towards the opposition was, at least to some extent, successful: people were anxious to keep their jobs, to avoid open confrontation with the authorities and to safeguard their little privileges.

The deterioration of the economic situation in the late nineteen-seventies changed the balance of forces considerably: shortages of consumer goods, lack of basic medicines, the collapse of the housing policy, long queues, humiliating negotiations with local authorities about services and housing repairs and, above all, inflation, resulted in panic buying and rocketing black-market prices. All this created a climate of nervousness and disappointment which made the criticism voiced by the opposition more and more impressive. The government was facing a dilemma: its credibility was crumbling, economic difficulties spoke for themselves, and the disparity between the rosy picture presented by the mass media and the grim realities that everybody faced, provoked the man in the street to express his discontent openly.

In these circumstances the opposition became a channel through which public discontent could be articulated and echoed publicly. With each passing month it became more and more difficult to silence the opposition. At the same time, resort to plain coercion would pose serious problems for the following reasons:

(1) Gierek's dependence on foreign credits which became in the last years of the nineteen-seventies the necessary condition for economic survival, made it practically impossible to launch a full-scale campaign against the political opposition. In a situation of growing discontent, such a campaign would have led to the arrest or internment of many well-known people and would have had grave repercussions in the West where Gierek's image as the liberal leader was his main trump card in securing further aid for the ailing economy.

(2) There were, however, deeper reasons for Gierek's indecisive approach in dealing with political unrest. He and his close associates knew only too well that the causes of the crisis went deeper than the outward expressions of ideological dissent on the part of a few thousand of the most defiant intellectuals. The looming crisis could not be solved by crushing the critics of the government. In 1968, Gomułka had approved a similar crusade against restive students and intellectuals, but this had not prevented the workers from taking to the streets two years later. This time the economic situation was much more serious and the response of the workers towards harsh measures on a massive scale were difficult to predict: they might turn against the party and give support to the dissidents.

(3) The apparent leniency of Gierek towards the opposition led to serious accusations against him from the hard-liners, many of whom did not grasp how far the crisis had advanced. They knew, however, that such a confrontation would reinforce their position which in turn made Gierek even more determined to stick to his moderate policy.

The conjunction of the economic and political crisis

affected even the party rank and file who resented the arbitrary rule within the party. The worsening economic situation was more and more often criticised in public by ordinary party members. The leadership was also criticised by the militia and other state functionaries, whose salaries did not catch up with inflationary price rises for many goods and who were affected by inadequate supplies of many basic goods in the state-controlled market. They were more and more convinced that the authorities were unable to deal with the economic and political situation.

People protested increasingly against the ineffectiveness, corruption and arbitrariness of the party–state administration, the privileged position of party and state officials and the blatant hypocrisy of official propaganda which unashamedly poured out lies about the economic situation.

The party was rapidly increasing in numbers but, as later events demonstrated, this became a source of weakness rather than strength in the relationship between the party and society. The ranks of the party were growing as follows (Staar, 1982, p.164):

1967 (May)	2,000,000
1970 (October)	2,296,000
1975 (November)	2,453,000
1980 (September)	3,158,000

Although Gierek and his associates were held responsible for all that happened in the nineteen-seventies, the whole party was under attack even from some of those who remained in its ranks.

The party members were those whose support brought Gierek to power on the basis of a programme which was supposed to produce an economic miracle. They agreed to suppress all dissenting voices and any sound criticism from the public. They built society's official image on shameless lies and were the guardians of corruption and inefficiency.

Inflation and shortages in the market affected the party–state administrators less than other groups of the population: they were the ones who distributed the goods and had access to scarce resources and were able to build up their

fortunes and power on the very difficulties which afflicted
the economy. Even those at the bottom of the bureaucratic
ladder, as sole distributors of dwindling resources, had more
opportunity and were more motivated to increase their own
share of benefits than ever before: peasants paid officials for
being allowed to buy coal and fertilisers; suppliers of
agricultural products paid inspectors for giving them good
prices for their products; managers were able to sell building
materials and sub-contract their own employees to work for
private entrepreneurs; public prosecutors were lavishly
rewarded for tolerating the malpractices of local dignitaries
and businessmen; bribed militia overlooked illegal transport
of cement and brick from building sites; directors of
department stores charged their customers extra for higher
quality goods, etc. Thousands of villas were erected in
provincial towns; state officials and public figures competed
with private entrepreneurs in displays of wealth. The scope
for corruption, servilism and total irresponsibility of party
and state functionaries regarding the most vital issues of
economic policy was undoubtedly the factor contributing to
the depth of the political crisis.

Parallel to this were abuses of the rights of ordinary
people at the local level. The situation in the provinces and
localities was worse than in Warsaw, with its multitude of
government and party institutions and greater openness to
the outside world.

All this meant that resentment was much deeper and more
widespread than in the earlier decade. The conjunction of
the economic with the political crisis was therefore the major
characteristic of the situation. A chasm developed between
ordinary people, whether party members or not, and those
state functionaries and members of the party organs who
were placed in good strategic positions to take advantage of
the system at the expense of their fellow citizens.

In a nationwide poll carried out by the Polish Academy of
Science, the peasants expressed their growing discontent
with the state bureaucracy by responding to the following
question: How do you assess the work of the following
groups of employees on a nationwide scale? The answers
were as follows:

Table 6·4 Question: How do you assess the work of the following groups?

	Peasants	Workers	Officials	Managerial staff Intermediary level	Higher level
Well	58.4	46.0	29.4	29.2	21.6
Medium	28.2	31.0	34.8	35.2	29.5
Badly	13.4	23.0	34.8	35.4	48.6

Source: Dziatłowicki (1981).

In 1981 when people in Gdańsk were asked about the cause of the outbreak of discontent in Poland in 1980, 56.7 per cent of respondents expressed the view that the causes were political and referred to the alienation of the authorities, their privileges, centralised decision-making, lack of credibility, corrupt practices, etc. Another 23.1 per cent referred to the social and economic circumstances and only 10.4 per cent saw the reasons for the troubles in purely economic terms (Latoszek, 1981).

The contrast with the circumstances which preceded Gomułka's downfall was therefore staggering. At that time criticism of the leader was mainly voiced by his party comrades and rivals who built up a case against his policies in a way which did not jeopardise the position of the party–state. This time, widespread discontent was directed against the ruling bureaucracies at all levels and was voiced by a disaffected public and rank-and-file party members.

In letters to the Deputy Prime Minister, Rakowski, on the occasion of his televised talks, we read:

I shall tell it briefly: our country was ruled by people deprived of all good qualities—thieves, blockheads, egoists, snobs and even beasts and other crooks. (Rakowski, 1981b, p.53)

We little people are not ruled by the Party or Government. We live under the thumb of bureaucratic despots for whom the highest orders are a mere alibi for their own stupid ideas, aiming exclusively at their self-interest and maximum comfort. (ibid., p.231)

It is high time that you beat your own chest simply because your party has ruined our economy and stolen what was there to steal. (ibid., p.272)

INTERNAL CONTRADICTIONS OF POLITICAL NORMALISATION—SOME CONCLUSIONS

A comparison between the causes and the outcomes of the 1970 and 1980 crises allows us to understand that the way the crisis in 1970 was solved made it impossible, or unlikely, that the same solution could be applied ten years later when the country was faced by a similar outbreak of mass discontent.

Apart from the economic stalemate which left no resources with which the economy could be stabilised and the crisis solved, political resources were also totally exhausted and confidence in the party to find a solution to the mounting difficulties was completely destroyed. The argument that those who had caused the trouble should not be trusted to put it right was often repeated. The expedient of changing the First Secretary as happened in 1956 and 1970 could not be successfully repeated since the party lacked any personality of national standing capable of inspiring respect and trust as a new leader. In such circumstances the chances for another political normalisation were practically non-existent; there was nothing to be offered in economic terms, people would not be placated by ritualistic manoeuvres and the rigidity of the party excluded the possibility of substantial political and social reforms to revive the economy.

A comparison between the situation in Poland, on the one hand, and Czechoslovakia and Hungary on the other, illustrates the complexity of the political situation faced by the Polish leadership in 1980.

In Czechoslovakia repressive measures against political dissent were combined with an improvement in living standards, while in Poland a relatively liberal policy seemed to be accompanied by an increasingly inefficient economic system.

In Hungary, Kadar's regime signified more and more a policy of retreat from the Stalinist past. As Kende points out (1982, pp.10-11):

1. the private life-sphere was restored to individuals;
2. the arbitrary power exercised by the police was reduced considerably;

3. the right of ownership of small property was gradually extended;
4. central planning was reduced in order to orient production according to demand as really manifested;
5. experts were currently in the majority among the managers;
6. contacts with the world were widened;
7. creative individuals enjoyed limited liberty.

In Poland similar changes had been implemented some to a much greater degree under Gomułka's regime. Under Gierek there was a retreat from many former liberal principles. Having failed to achieve the great leap in the economic sphere, the government was blamed at the same time for its neo-Stalinist endeavours. A restrained attitude towards the opposition was perceived in those circumstances not as evidence of democratic policy but as a sign of weakness and lack of resolve in pursuing the party line. While in Hungary and Czechoslovakia the authorities inspired fear, in Poland they were treated with growing contempt and complacency. Concessions on which Gierek relied as a last resort therefore proved less and less effective at a time when the economic situation was deteriorating alarmingly.

In the year of the outbreak of the workers' resistance, economic conditions in Poland were judged to be bad by the following percentages of the population: in February 1980, 46 per cent; in July, 65 per cent; in September, 86 per cent; and in October, 96 per cent (Kurczewski, 1981).

In a democratic society the crisis could have been solved by general elections and by a party or parties in opposition taking over the government. In a one-party system such institutional means do not exist. Coercion became imperative to restore order against the militant masses aiming for a head-on confrontation with a regime they despised and hated.

Paradoxically enough, the desperate economic situation which had triggered the outbreak of the political crisis, later became a powerful argument of official propaganda against the mass movement. It became obvious that the growing economic crisis, the catastrophic collapse of production, rising inflation and shortages of food, fuel and basic industrial consumer products called for drastic measures backed by the entire coercive power of the Communist state.

A graphic presentation of the economic crisis illustrates not only the staggering collapse of Poland's economy but the ordeal of its subsequent recovery.

% change on previous year

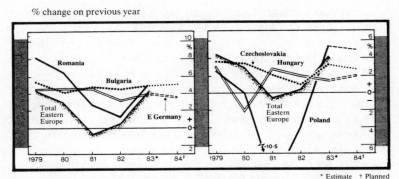

* Estimate   † Planned

Figure 6·1: Industrial production in Eastern Europe

Sources: ECE National Reports (Figure taken from *The Economist*, 17 December 1983.)

Coercion was to become a stabilising factor and a method of achieving economic reconstruction. The military government which replaced party rule in December 1981 was a method of achieving the transition which could and would not be implemented this time by political means. The appearances of legitimacy based on consensus disappeared and the party–state had to declare that naked power was the foundation of Communist rule in the country. This was in contrast to the early years of Communist power when the struggle against counter-revolutionary forces was the regime's justification for its use of coercive measures. The new situation required the use of coercion against society which was claiming its rights from the conservative establishment.

The military coup was justified by the Polish leadership by

pointing to the catastrophe which would inevitably have befallen the country if the Solidarity movement had prevailed; as Jaruzelski argued, Russian intervention and civil war were unavoidable if the army had waited any longer.

What might have happened is of course open to speculation. There is no point in trying to answer this question which, though arousing passionate controversies can never be solved. The most characteristic aspect of this development is that of the use of direct coercion in solving the crisis. Once more the party–state bureaucracy saw no other way but to resort to overt force.

7 Conclusions— Revolution, counter-revolution and the coercive state

A comparison between the major political crises in Poland in 1956, 1970 and 1980–1 reveals important differences:

(1) In 1956 the mass movement was dominated politically and ideologically by the reformist and revisionist faction within the party. In 1970 the movement erupted spontaneously among factory workers but they addressed the party as the legitimate authority who they expected to deal with their grievances and demands. In 1980–1 the mass movement developed not only outside the party but against the party; it was building an ideological and political identity of its own and regarded the party as an alien and hostile force.

(2) In 1956 the only institutional structures created by the mass movement were a number of clubs of the intelligentsia and autonomous workers' councils, which emerged in several factories. All of these were liquidated in one way or another in Gomułka's first years. In 1970 the strike committees were the sole institutional expression of the movement. They were of even shorter duration and disappeared when the strikes were called off.

In 1980–1 local and national institutions emerged: the NSZZ *Solidarność* (the capitals stand for Independent Self-managing Trade Union) with its elaborate territorial structure and, somewhat later, Rural Solidarity, a farmers' union. Their numerical strength, the scope of their activities and the pervasiveness of their influence made these unions an institution able to match and counteract not only Communist industrial management but also the Communist state.

(3) In 1956 centralised ideological control was seriously challenged by the growing independence of many editorial boards, by the lack of control over party meetings and mass rallies, but the mass movement never reached a point where

it would be able to develop a media network of its own.

In 1970 the local strike committees relied on loudspeakers installed in their factories. In 1980–1 a point was reached when the central monopoly of the mass media virtually disappeared: Solidarity was publishing dailies and weeklies of its own, central bulletins were circulating through the union's internal network, and innumerable local publications were mushrooming.

(4) Many of the differences mentioned above are due to the fact that in contrast to 1955–6 and 1970 the attempts to end the political crisis of 1980 at a relatively early stage proved unsuccessful. While in 1956 the rise of Gomułka halted the developing mass movement, and in 1970 economic concessions were sufficient to defuse the workers' protest, in 1980–1 the movement was able to gather momentum; it passed the stage of scattered strikes, it developed into protracted sit-ins, and once the new independent nationwide union was created it generated a political and social mass movement on an unprecedented scale.

In view of the scope of the movement of 1980–1, the forces it mobilised, the programme it developed, and the changes it was able to enforce, it is more appropriate to speak of a revolution rather than a political crisis. The impetus for that revolution derived at first from the very strategy of the authorities who tried in the summer of 1980 to nip the protest movement in the bud by conceding the wage demands of the striking workers in different factories in the vain hope that the fire of industrial unrest would not spread. The net result of those endeavours was to stimulate workers in other factories to make similar and further demands. The turning-point was reached when the authorities agreed to let the workers in Gdańsk create a free. independent, self-managing trade union. Once the convenors of the new union decided to form it on a national scale, the many separate streams of protest were brought together in a matter of weeks and combined into the huge 'Solidarity' organisation. The response of the party leadership at that stage was ambiguous; there is no doubt that some party leaders believed that mass access of party members and activists to Solidarity would help to swamp the new union, giving the party a chance to recover some lost ground. Whole factories, including their managements, were thus declaring their allegiance to Solidarity and within weeks the new organisation numbered several million people.

Did the Polish revolution have any chance of achieving its objectives? Past experience would suggest a typology, such as the following, of different scenarios in solving political crises and dealing with protest movements in Eastern Europe:

Table 7·1 Scenarios of political crises in Eastern Europe

Responses of the ruling elite	Mass movement demands	
	Moderate	*Extreme*
No concessions	Suppression *(Germany 1953)* or Trade-off *(Poland 1970)* or Escalation *(Poland 1980)*	Confrontation and intervention *(Hungary 1956)*
Some concessions	Co-operation *(Poland 1956)*	Confrontation *(Poland 1981)*
Essential Systemic transformations	Intervention *(Czechoslovakia 1968)*	Intervention or ?

The table illustrates, albeit in a very schematic way, various combinations in which mass protest and ruling-party policy do interact and the impact of those interactions on the outcome of the crises. The dependence of that outcome on a single external factor, that is, the military power of the USSR to intervene and invade the satellite countries whenever she deems it necessary for the stabilisation of the Communist bloc, is more than obvious.

The case of Hungary in 1956 shows that such an intervention occurred when the masses took to the streets and the apparatus of the Communist State was powerless to resist. The case of Czechoslovakia was an example of intervention when the party leadership had gone so far in their reformist endeavours that, in the Soviet view, their policy threatened the foundations of the system. The case of Poland in 1970 was an example of a peaceful solution of a crisis based on a trade-off of economic concessions for an undertaking from the workers to refrain from further demands.

The case of Poland in 1956 is most interesting because it represented a very peculiar combination of moderate demands and self-restraint on the part of the people, together with the willingness of the party to carry out limited but effective reforms. Both factors contributed to a peaceful solution which protected Poland from the possible recurrence of the Hungarian or the future Czechoslovak scenario.

In 1981 it was obvious that none of the above-mentioned combinations would be effective. A compromise solution of the kind similar to 1956 was most unlikely to occur. In 1981 the two factors of crucial importance were the economic crisis and party policy; of those two the economic crisis was foremost. The overall character of that crisis left no room for manoeuvre, hence no trade-off similar to that in 1970 was possible. Harsh austerity measures were unavoidable, but the longer the political crisis lasted the less chance there was that society would accept such measures of its own accord. The following points illustrate the situation at that time.

a) The wave of new demands encompassed not only further pay concessions but were extended to many different social benefits which the state was unable to provide.

b) One of the major problems solved by government concessions was the granting of free Saturdays. At a time of a dramatic drop in production the shortening of the working week contributed to further imbalance in the economy.

c) The militancy of the miners posed a serious problem for the balance of payments. At a time when most credits were brought to an end and industry suffered more and more drastic power cuts the miners were able to obtain further concessions which in fact reduced production in the mining industry.

d) Other vital exports, for example of food and in particular high-quality meat, were hindered by a refusal of the dockers to load the ships. The public supported the resolve that no food should be exported from Poland as long as the country suffered from food shortages.

Within months the economic situation had deteriorated to the point where economists started to give warnings about the imminent collapse of the economy. The shops were virtually empty. People were queueing day and night to buy basic foods. Peasants reduced the sale of their products to the state, more and more often they demanded payments in foreign currency from their private customers, and the black-market prices of all commodities shot up to new heights. Factories started organising supplies for their employees by swapping product for product. Local administrators introduced unofficial systems of food rationing. A general feeling of uncertainty and the spread of wild rumours aggravated the situation. People expected a currency devaluation and were desperately trying to get rid of their 'empty money'. Panic buying developed on a massive scale: people were spending their money on anything they could get hold of, and as a result even products which were otherwise in sufficient supply were sold out as soon as they appeared in the shops. Organised gangs besieged shops, buying more expensive items such as carpets, crystal or refrigerators in the hope of reselling them at inflated black-market prices.

A good illustration of the hyperinflation which developed in 1981 was the black-market price of American dollars:

Table 7·2 Black-market price of American dollars in Poland 1971–81

Year	Price paid for one dollar in zloty
1971	94
1975	113
1980	134
1981	900

Source: Życie Gosprodarcze, 23–30 December 1984, p.3).

The government was blamed for everything. People were convinced that the catastrophe could have been averted: the fact that it was not must either be because of the ineptitude of the authorities or because of their policy of hoarding goods in order to starve the population into surrender.

All attempts to restore some balance of the economy by the regulation of the money supply, raising some prices and restraining wage demands depended on the approval of Solidarity. Yet Solidarity demanded further political concessions in return for their co-operation. Their leaders rightly argued that the masses were not prepared to endure harsh economic measures without getting something in return. At an advanced stage of the economic crisis access to the mass media and control of the distribution of food by Solidarity became the stumbling block to any further economic negotiations.

One could ask why the party leaders did not look for a political trade-off which might have appeased the movement. The answer is to be sought in the situation within the party, its ossification being another factor which significantly influenced the outcome of the crisis. The party after 1968 had purged all reformists so efficiently that when the time came that they were badly needed, the only candidate to conduct significant negotiations with Solidarity was Kania, formerly responsible for the Security Police and at best a cautious and pragmatic bureaucrat. The party apparatus from top to bottom remained rigid in its position of political conservatism.

Faced by the upsurge of the Solidarity movement the party did its best to oppose the movement as far as it could. Unable to win any battles in a frontal attack they supported and tacitly encouraged the resistance to Solidarity demands at the local level. The net result of this policy was further escalation of the conflict and increasing militancy of the movement. The regional activists of Solidarity were in the forefront of interminable squabbles with the local party–state bosses. Some of these struggles were elevated to the status of a *cause célèbre* of the whole movement.

The top of the party hierarchy oscillated between the choice of hard-line and moderate policies to contain the

Solidarity movement, but there was no single attempt to come forward with any political reforms which would allow it to institutionalise the economic and social conflicts.

These two factors, that is, the depth of the economic crisis and the policy of the party, accounted for the inevitable escalation of mass discontent and precluded any compromise in solving the crisis.

Two important congresses took a characteristic stance: the Party Congress which revealed that the party as a whole was not prepared to meet the demands of Solidarity; and the Congress of Solidarity which revealed the unbridgeable gap between the grass-root militants and the concessions the party leadership was prepared to negotiate.

As far as Solidarity's First National Congress was concerned, the moderate leaders of the movement stood no chance of surviving the electoral onslaught and it was only by adopting a militant stance that Watęsa was able to retain his personal influence throughout the autumn of 1981.

The dynamics of the relationship between the Communist establishment and the Solidarity movement led inexorably to the polarisation and intensification of the conflict. A simple scheme illustrates that development. By taking as significant indicators the escalation of demands by the protest movement and the concessions (or lack of concessions) to those demands by the authorities we are able to depict the development of the political situation as follows:

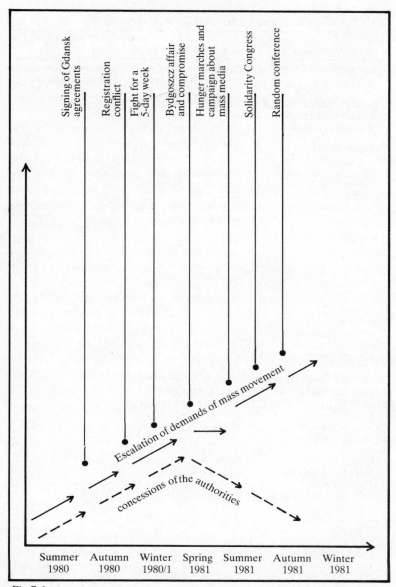

Fig 7·1

The above figure can be substantiated by a list of events which were significant in the escalation of the conflict.

Table 7.3 The escalation of the conflict in Poland in 1980–81

	Mass movement	Government policies	Other important events
Summer 1980	Localised strikes in July	Pay rises in Lublin and Radom, 20, 21 July	Moscow Olympics, 19 July–3 August
	Strikes in Gdańsk and Szczecin, August. Workers present to government list of 21 demands, 23 August	Gdańsk negotiations, August 14–31. Szczecin negotiations, 19–30 August	
	Strike spreads to Silesian coalfields, 28 August	The Szczecin and Gdańsk agreements, 31 August Jasrezebie agreement with miners, 3 September	Kania replaces Gierek as Party First Secretary, 5 September
		Declaration that agreements apply to the whole country, 15 September	
Autumn 1980	Gdańsk meeting of regional unions establishes *Solidarność*, 22 September		
	Denial of registration of Solidarity unless it explicitly recognizes the Party's leading role – crisis, 24 September–10 November	Supreme Court rules Solidarity may be registered without changing its charter, 10 November	
	Crisis: Printer Narożniak arrested after classified document on ways of suppressing dissent leaked, 20–24 November	Narożniak released, 24 November	
	Farmers meet in Warsaw, demand creation of Rural Solidarity, 14 December		Soviet military manoeuvres around Poland's borders, 1–13 December.

1970 Martyrs' memorial dedicated in Gdańsk in presence of leaders of Solidarity, Church and government, 16 December

Mass movement	Government policies	Other important events
Solidarity demands five-day week, January	Compromise agreement on five-day week, 30 January	

90 day industrial truce proclaimed, 9 February

Winter 1981

First Congress of Rural Solidarity in Poznań, 8 March		Defence minister General Jaruzelski becomes Prime Minister, 9 February
		26th Congress of the CPSU meets in Moscow, 23 February–3 March
		Soviet–Polish meeting in Moscow demands reversal of the course of events in Poland, 4 March

Spring 1981

Violent break-up of Solidarity meeting in Bydgoszcz by police 19 March, followed by period of tension, 20–30 March, 4-hour warning strike, 27 March and threat of general strike. Punishment of those responsible for violence demanded	Wałęsa–Rakowski compromise on Bydgoszcz affair, 30 March	*Soyuz '81* Warsaw pact manoeuvres in Poland, GDR, the USSR and Czechoslovakia, 18 March–7 April 1981
	Meat rationing begins, 1 April	Soviet Politburo member and Party Secretary Mikhail Suslov visits Poland, holds talks with Polish leaders, 23 April
	Rationing extended to other products, 1 May	
Solidarity backs down on demand of punishment, 30 March	Rural Solidarity registered by Warsaw court, 12 May	
		Primate Wyszyński dies, 28 May

Unrest in the country, highlighted by clash between crowd and police in Otwock, 8 May and defacing of Soviet war memorial in Lublin, 13 June

Food protests throughout Poland, 25 July–20 August	Extra-ordinary Congress of the PUWP, 14–20 July	Archbishop Józef Glemp appointed Primate, 7 July

	Mass movement	Government policies	Other important events
Summer 1981	Print workers strike in protest against regime's propaganda campaign against Solidarity, 18–19 August	Regime's propaganda offensive against Solidarity, July–August	
	First session of Solidarity National Congress in Gdańsk, 5–10 September. Message 'to the working people in Eastern Europe' adopted, 8 September	Propaganda campaign against Solidarity escalates, especially against message 'to the working people of Eastern Europe', September	*Zapad-81* manoeuvres and Soviet navy war games off Poland's Baltic coast, 4–12 September Angry reaction from the USSR and other Soviet bloc countries to message 'to the working people of Eastern Europe' from 10 September Letter from Soviet Party and State Leaders to Polish leaders demands 'to cut short hostile campaign against the USSR', 18 September
Autumn 1981	Second session of Solidarity National Congress in Gdańsk, 26 September–7 October	Government decides to extend conscripts' service in the army by two months, 16 October	
	Unrest and strikes all over Poland, September – November, including strikes by miners, strikes over food supplies, 8–13 October and general strike in Zielona Góra province,	General Jaruzelski becomes First Secretary of the PUWP CC, retains the offices of defence minister and prime minister, 18 October	
	22 October–13 November	Government – Solidarity talks on prices, 15–18 October	

	Mass movement	Government policies	Other important events
		Jaruzelski, Glemp and Wałęsa meet, discuss setting up of 'front of national accord', 4 November	
	Cadets of Fire Brigade College hold sit-in strike, 25 November. College cleared by police, 2 December	Government–Solidarity talks on economic reforms, 17, 19 and 26–27 November	
		PUWP CC Plenum passes hard-line resolution: 'no act against . . . the political system . . . can be tolerated', 27–28 November	
Autumn 1981		Price rises of petrol and diesel-oil, 22 November, of spirits and beer, 1 December	
	Solidarity leadership meets in Radom, 3 December, protests against government actions, warns Solidarity will respond with 24-hour general strike to introduction of extraordinary measures		Warsaw Pact foreign ministers meet in Bucharest, 1–2 December
			Warsaw Pact defence ministers meet in Moscow, 1–4 December
	Mazowsze branch of Solidarity meets, 6 December, proclaims 17 December day of protest against police actions		
	Solidarity National Committee meets in Gdańsk shipyard, 11–12 December, radical demands including free elections and referendum voiced	Imposition of martial law, 13 December	

To summarise: the authorities were not able to cope with the economic crisis as long as the political crisis was developing. And a peaceful solution of the political crisis was at least partly prevented by the aggravation of the economic situation.

The solution was understandably sought in the application of direct coercion. Although the presence of the coercive state was hardly noticeable during the numerous conflicts between Solidarity and the authorities, the machinery of coercion, that is, the army, the political police and the combat units of ordinary police remained intact and ready to act when necessary. Their existence was easily overlooked by many who relied on the numerical superiority of the Solidarity movement. Whenever references to coercion were made, they were taken to apply primarily to an exterior force, i.e., the Soviet army; its readiness to intervene if things in Poland went too far was widely recognised. One ignored to a large extent the power of the Polish army and police units, the superiority of their equipment and training and the role of organisation and discipline.

When the coup took place the functions of naked power in solving the political crisis and dealing with the economic problems became obvious. There is no doubt that the command economy would have collapsed if the state had not used its powers of intervention.

The circumstances in which the military coup in Poland took place corroborates Kerr's thesis (discussed in Chapter 1) that in a case of negative economic growth oppressive power becomes an indispensable instrument of integrating and controlling society.

One could argue that a system relying on the sheer use of force cannot last; social life implies cooperation which cannot be achieved when social consensus is lacking. It would follow that the use of direct coercion removes the chances of effective cooperation and is therefore self-defeating.

The development of the economic and political situation in Poland does not confirm such conclusions. As has been indicated elsewhere, the system has built-in mechanisms which legitimise the rule of those who occupy the positions of power.

Gilison (1972, p.9) has enumerated five conditions on which the legitimacy of governments rests:

1) They are reasonably efficient in performing economic and other functions.

2) They retain control of important components of the political system over time.

3) They generally conform to prevailing social values.

4) They use educational systems and mass media to inculcate supportive values.

5) They are sufficiently responsive to the needs of subjects.

There is no doubt that at least by some accounts Jaruzelski's regime meets these requirements. The prophets of doom seem to ignore the fact that once a society is put on the path of a command economy it has to accept any government which is able to carry out the functions of centralised management because in such a system any government is better than no government (or a weak government, for that matter). People have to rely on the bureaucratic apparatus to organise work, to provide services, to get the commodities they need, to utilise existing resources and to ensure at least some stability and security. Whoever is in charge of that apparatus will sooner or later be accepted in his managerial and administrative role. A revolt which is not able to transform the nature of society leaves people empty-handed; the bureaucratic élite re-emerges as the only integrating and activating force of social activities. They may defy many accepted social values and ignore, even suppress, the higher needs of their subjects, as long as they can utilise the basic instinct of self-preservation. There is no doubt that such an instinct is particularly strong when people are faced with a deep economic crisis.

As far as Poland is concerned the bureaucratic Leviathan is, however, back with a difference. Its nature and the coercive foundations of its power cannot remain cloaked any longer, and thus demystification becomes a vital ingredient of political reality.

Select bibliography and references

Allard, E. and W. Wesołowski (eds) (1978), *Social Structure and Change: Finland and Poland, Comparative Perspective*. Warsaw: Polish Scientific Publishers.

Andrzejewicz, Z. (1979), 'Dochody ludności rolniczej z produkcji rolnej oraz z pozostałych zródeł', *Wieś i Rolnictwo*, no.2.

The Anti-Jewish Campaign in Present-day Poland (1968), London: Institute of Jewish Affairs.

'Anti-Semitism without Jews' (1979), Czechoslovakia *RFE* Research*, Situation Report, Czechoslovakia, 14 January.

*RFE—Radio Free Europe.

Ascherson, N. (1981), *The Polish August*, Harmondsworth: Penguin.

Ash, Garton T. (1983), *The Polish Revolution, Solidarity 1980–82*, London: Jonathan Cape.

Asmus, R. D. (1982), 'Supply shortages in the GDR', *RFE Research*, Background Report/235, GDR, 10 December.

Babiuch, E. (1980), 'Exposé', *Nowe Drogi*, no.4, April.

Bachrach, S. A. and E. J. Lawler (1981), *Power and Politics in Organizations*, San Francisco, Jossey-Bass Publishers.

Bahro, R. (1981), *The Alternative in Eastern Europe*, London: Verso.

Banaś, J. (1979), *The Scapegoats. The Exodus of Remnants of Polish Jewry*, London: Weidenfeld & Nicolson.

Banaszkiewicz, B. (1980), 'O właściwą rangę zawodu rolnika', *Tygodnik Powszechny*, 28 September.

Bauman, Z. (1971), 'Twenty years after: the crisis of Soviet-type societies', *Problems of Communism*, November–December.

Bertsch, G. *et al.* (1982), *Comparing Political Systems: Power and Policy in Three Worlds*, New York: Wiley.

Beskid, Lidia (1977), *Konsumpcja w rodzinach pracowniczych*, Warsaw: PWE.

——— (1978), 'Tendencje i wzory konsumpcji', *Nowe Drogi*, no.6, June.

——— (1980), 'Potrzeby ludności w świetle badań społecznych', *Nowe Drogi*, no.6, June.

——— (1982), 'Pay and income as factors in the crisis' in *Crises and Conflicts. See Crises and Conflicts*.

Bielasiak, J. (1981), 'Recruitment policy, élite integration and political stability in People's Poland' in *Background to Crisis:*

Policy and Poli.
1981.

——— (1983), 'The p̶̶̶̶̶
a Revolution. See Bru.

Bieṅkowski, Władysław (
partyjnego sumienia', *Aspo*

Binder, L. *et al.* (1971), *Cri.*
Development, Princeton: Princ

Błaszczyk, B. (1983),Uspo₁
społecznogospodarczego in *Demoknd. Genesis of*
Morawski 1983b.

Blażyca, G. (1982), 'The degeneration oı
Poland' in *Policy and Politics in Contempora.*
Failure and Crisis. See Woodall 1982.

Błażynski, G. (1979), *Flashpoint Poland*, New Yc
Press.

Bobrowski, Cz. (1980), 'Raport do kosza', *Życie Gospe* ͅ ͅ ͅe, 7
December.

——— (1981), 'Raport o stanie gospodarki', *Życie Gospodarcze*,
14 June.

Bogacz, J. (1980), 'Dwuzawodowi producenci żywności', *Życie i*
Nowoczesność, 9 October.

Bogus, A. (1975), 'Dochody różnych grup pracowników z
zakładowych świadczeń socjalnych', *Praca i Zabezpieczenie*
Społeczne, no.10.

Boiter, A. (1964), 'When the kettle boils over', *Problems of*
Communism, January–February.

Bojko, L. (1980), 'Pogoda dla rolników', *Kultura*, 19 October.

——— (1981), 'Czas chłopów', *Polityka*, 28 March.

Bombera, Z. (1980), 'Teoria ekonomiczna socjalizmu a rozwój
społeczno-gospodarczy Polski', *Nowe Drogi*, no.12 December.

Bornstein, M. (ed.) (1973), *Plan and Market: Economic Reform in*
Eastern Europe, Stanford: Yale University Press.

Bromke, A. (1978a), 'The opposition in Poland' in *Problems of*
Communism, September–October.

——— (1978b), 'Czechoslovakia 1968 and Poland 1978: a dilemma
for Moscow' in *International Journal*, Autumn.

Bromke, A. and T. Rakowska–Harmstone (eds) (1972), *The*
Communist States in Disarray, Minneapolis: University of
Minnesota Press.

Bromke, A. and J. W. Strong (eds) (1973), *Gierek's Poland*, New
York: Preager Publishers.

Brown, A. (1979), 'Eastern Europe: 1968, 1978, 1998', *Daedalus*,
Winter.

205

9), _Political Culture and_
Party States, London: Mac-

impact of international stagflation on
changes in East Europe: theoretical
cInnes _et al._, _The Soviet Union and East_
_1980s_, Oakville, Ont.: Mosaic Press.
raham (ed.) (1983), _Poland. Genesis of a Revolu-_
w York: Vintage Books.
. (1969), _The Economics and Politics of Socialism_,
ondon: Routledge and Kegan Paul.

—— (1975a), _Socialist Ownership and Political Systems_, London: Routledge and Kegan Paul.

—— (1975b), _The Economics and Politics of Socialism_, London: Routledge and Kegan Paul.

—— (1979), 'The East European Reforms: What happened to them?', _Soviet Studies_, April.

—— (1980a), 'The economic role of the state: West and East', _Survey_, Autumn.

—— (1980b), 'Political systems and economic efficiency: the East European context', _Journal of Comparative Economics_, March.

—— (1983a), 'Political pluralism and markets in Communist systems' in S. G. Solomon (ed.), _Pluralism in the Soviet Union_, London: Macmillan.

—— (1983b), 'Economics and politics: the fatal link' in _Poland. Genesis of a Revolution. See_ Brumberg 1983.

Brus, W., P. Kende and Z. Mlynar (1982), 'Normalisation Process in Soviet Dominated Central Europe, Hungary, Czechoslovakia, Poland', Study no.1., Research project 'Crisis in Soviet-type systems'.

Bunce V. and J. M. Echols (1978), 'Power and policy in Communist systems: the problem of incrementalism', _Journal of Politics_, vol. 40.

Burks, R. V. (1965), _·The Dynamics of Communism in Eastern Europe_, Princeton: Princeton University Press.

—— (1973), 'The political implications of economic reform' in _Plan and Market: Economic Reform in Eastern Europe. See_ Bernstein 1973.

Bywalec, Cz. (1980), 'O dochodach i konsumpcji', _Życie Literackie_, 4 May.

Chęciński, M. (1982), _Poland: Communism, Nationalism, Antisemitism_, New York: Karz–Cohl Publishers.

Chrypiński, (1981), 'Church and state in Gierek's Poland', in

Background to Crisis: Policy Politics in Gierek's Poland. See Simon and Kanet 1981.

Cieplak, T. N. (1974), 'Some distinctive characteristics of the Communist system in the Polish People's Republic', in *The Polish Review*, vol. XIX, no.1.

Connor, W. D. (1977), 'Social change and stability in Eastern Europe', *Problems of Communism*, November–December.

—— (1979), *Socialism, Politics and Equality. Hierarchy and Change in Eastern Europe and the USSR*, New York: Columbia University Press.

—— (1980), 'Dissent in Eastern Europe: a new coalition?' in *Problems of Communism*, January–February.

Coser, L. A. (1962), *Continuities in the Study of Social Conflict*, London: Collier-Macmillan.

Crises and Conflicts. The Case of Poland 1980–1981, (1982), Sisyphus Sociological Studies, vol. III, Warsaw: PWN.

Czarna Ksiega Cenzury PRL (1978 and 1979), London: Aneks Publishers.

Dąbkowski, A. (1981), 'Czy luka inflacyjna sięgnie 1000 miliardów zł?' in *Kierunki*, 8 March.

Danecki, J. (ed.) (1980), *Towards Poland 2000. Problems of Social Development*, Warsaw: Zakład im. Ossolińskich.

Davis, N. (1981), *God's Playground. A History of Poland*, 2 vols, Oxford: Clarendon Press.

Dawisha, K. and Ph. Hanson, (eds) (1981), *Soviet–East European Dilemmas*, London: Heinemann for the Royal Institute of International Affairs.

Dissent in Poland, Reports / and Documents in Translation, December 1975–July 1977, (1979), London: Association of Polish Students and Graduates in Exile.

Djilas, M. (1966), *The New Class*, London: Unwin Books.

Dorn, Ludwik (1981), 'Konflikt', *Rzeczpospolita Polska*, no.2, February.

Drewnowski, J. (ed.) (1982), *Crisis in the East-European Economies: The Spread of the Polish Disease*, London: Croom Helm.

Drożej i gorzej (1983). *Rzeczpospolita*, 26 July.

Dziatłowicki, J. (1981), 'Poglądy wsi', *Polityka*, 7 March.

Dziewanowski, M. K. (1976), *The Communist Party of Poland*, Cambridge, Mass: Harvard University Press.

—— (1977), *Poland in the 20th Century*, New York: Columbia University Press.

Faber, B. (ed.) (1976), *The Social Structure of Eastern Europe*, London: Praeger Publishers.

Fallenbuchl, Z. M. (1970), 'The Communist pattern of industrialism', *Soviet Studies*, April.

———— (1973), 'The strategy of development and Gierek's economic manoeuvre' in *Gierek's Poland. See* Bromke and Strong 1973.

———— (1980), 'Pożyczki zachodnie dla PRL', *Kultura*, no.12.

———— (1982), 'Poland's economic crisis', *Problems of Communism*, March–April.

Fejtő, F. (1971), *A History of the People's Democracies: Eastern Europe since Stalin*, London: Pall Mall Press.

Field, M. G. (ed.) (1976), *Social Consequences of Modernisation in Communist Societies*, Baltimore: Johns Hopkins University Press.

Fireside, H. (1977), 'Détente and Soviet dissidents, A review article' in *Problems of Communism*, March–April.

Fischer–Galati, S. (ed.) (1981), *Eastern Europe in the 1980s*, London: Croom Helm.

Gabor, J. R. and P. Galasi (1978), 'Economic and sociological questions of the secondary economy—the private sphere under socialism', *Szociologia*, VII–IX, ref. in Hungary RFE Research, 6 July 1979.

Gamarnikow, M. (1972), 'Poland: on again—off again', in L. Delllin & H. Gross (eds), *Reforms in the Soviet and East European Economies*, Lexington, Mass.: Lexington Books.

Gati, Ch. (ed.) (1974), *The Politics of Modernisation in Eastern Europe*, London: Praeger Publishers.

Gidwitz, Betsy (1982), 'Labour unrest in the Soviet Union', *Problems of Communism*, November–December.

Gilison, J. (1972), *British and Soviet Politics: Legitimacy and Convergence*, Baltimore: Johns Hopkins University Press.

Gitelman, Z. (1981), 'The politics of socialist restoration', *Comparative Politics*, January.

Główczyk, J. (1981), 'Granice socjalistycznej odnowy', *Życie Gospodarcze*, 21 June.

Golan, G. (1971), *The Czechoslovak reform movement. Communism in Crisis, 1962-68*, London: Cambridge University Press.

Goldman, J. (1964), 'Fluctuations and trends in the rate of economics growth in some socialist countries' in *Economics of Planning*, no.2.

Gomułka, Stanislaw (1977), 'Economic factors in the democratisation of socialism and socialisation of capitalism', in *Journal of Comparative Economics*, 1.

———— (1978), 'Growth and the import of technology: Poland 1971–1980', *Cambridge Journal of Economics*, no.2.

———— (1983a), 'Specific and systemic causes of the Polish crisis

1980–1982', *Slavic and East European Studies*, Tel Aviv University.

——— (1983b), 'Industralization and the rate of growth: Eastern Europe 1955–75' in *Journal of Post-Keynesian Economics*, vol.V (3).

——— (1984a), *Poland's Industralization*, International Conference, Yale University, New Haven, USA, 22–25 May.

——— (1984b), 'The incompatibility of socialism and rapid innovation', *The Millenium Journal of International Studies*, vol. 13 (1).

Gościński, H. *et al.*, (1981), 'Rzecz o produkcji kryzysów', *Życie i Nowoczesność*, 26 February, 5 March, 19 March 1981.

'Gospodarka w nomenklaturze', (1981), A discussion organised by *Życie i Nowoczesność*, *Życie i Nowoczesność*, 16 April.

Gregory, P. and. G. Leptin, 'Similar Societies under differing economic systems: the case of the two Germanys', *Soviet Studies*, October.

Grochowski, Z. (1980), 'Skąd wziąć zboże i mięso', *Życie Gospodarcze*, 12 October.

Grossman, G. (1963), 'Notes for a theory of the command economy', *Soviet Studies*, April.

——— (1966), 'Gold and sword. Money in the Soviet command economy' in H. Rosovsky (ed.), *Industrialisation in Two Systems: Essays in Honour of Alexander Gerschenkron*, New York: Wiley.

——— (1977), 'The "second economy" of the USSR', *Problems of Communism*, September–October.

Hanson, P. (1978), 'Mieczkowski on consumption and politics: a comment', *Soviet Studies*, October.

Hare, P. (1983), 'The beginning of institutional reform in Hungary', *Soviet Studies*, July.

Hare, P. *et al.*, (1981), *Hungary: A Decade of Economic Reform*, London: George Allen & Unwin.

Hare, P. and P. Wanless (1981), 'Polish and Hungarian Economic Reforms', *Soviet Studies*, October.

Harman, Ch. (1974), *Bureaucracy and Revolution in Eastern Europe*, London: Pluto Press.

Hayek, F. A. (1976), *The Road to Serfdom*, London and Henley: Routledge & Kegan Paul.

Hayward J. and R. Barki (eds) (1979), *State and Society in Contemporary Europe*, Oxford: Martin Robertson.

Heidentraimer, Arnold J. (ed.) (1970), *Political Corruption. Readings in Comparative Analysis*, New York: Holt, Rinehart.

Herer, W. and W. Sadowski (1983), 'Czy rozumiemy własną

gospodarkę', *Życie Gospodarcze*, 5 June.
Hirszowicz, L. (1980), 'The current Polish crisis and the 1968 antisemitic campaign', *Research Report*, no.23, London: Institute of Jewish Affairs.
―――― (1981), 'Jewish themes in the Polish crisis', *Research Report*, nos.10 and 11, August; London: Institute of Jewish Affairs.
Hirszowicz, L. and T. Szafar (1977a), 'The Jewish scapegoat in Eastern Europe', *Patterns of Prejudice*, vol. II, no.5.
―――― and ―――― (1977b), 'Anti-Jewish themes in East-European Propaganda', *Research Report*, London: Institute of Jewish Affairs.
Hirszowicz, M. (1981), *The Bureaucratic Leviathan*, Oxford: Martin Robertson.
Hiscocks, R. (1963), *Poland. Bridge for the Abyss?* London: Oxford University Press.
Hőhman, A. (1982), *The East European Economies in the 1970s*, London: Butterworth.
Holzer, J. (1981), 'Doświadczenia marca 68', *Kierunki*, 17 May.
Horvat, B. (1982), *The Political Economy of Socialism: A Marxist Social Theory*, Oxford: Martin Robertson.
'Informacja o przebiegu i tle wydarzeń strajkowych' (1980), *Nowe Drogi*, nos.10–11, October–November.
International Labour Organization (1980), *Yearbook of Labour Statistics 1979*, Geneva: International Labour Office.
'Jeśli chodzi o ryj' (1974), *Polityka*, 12 October.
Johnson, C. (ed.) (1974), *Change in Communist System*, Englewood Cliffs, NJ: Prentice Hall.
Jones, Ch. D. (1977), 'Soviet hegemony in East Europe: the dynamics of political autonomy and military intervention', *World Politics*, XXIV.
Jonescu, G. (1967), *The Politics of the European Communist States*, London: Weidenfeld and Nicolson.
Jordan, Z. (ed.) (1971), *Karl Marx. Economy, Class and Social Revolution*, London: Nelson.
Jowitt, K. (1971), 'The concepts of liberalisation, integration and rationalisation in the course of East European development', *Studies in Comparative Communism*, April.
―――― (1983), 'Soviet neotraditionalism: the political corruption of a Leninist regime', *Soviet Studies*, July.
Józefiak, C. (1980). 'Nauki z historii reform', *Literatura*, 11 December.
Kabaj, M. (1980), 'Efektywność wzrostu płac', *Nowe Drogi*, February.

Kamiński, A. Z. (1983), 'Niedialektyczna koncepcja planowania i interes społeczny' in *Demokracja i gospodarka*. *See* Morawski 1983b.

Karol, K. (1959), *Visa for Poland*, London: MacGibbon and Kee.

Karpinski, J. (1980), 'Workers versus the Party–State in Poland', in *Freedom at Issue*, November and December.

—— (1982), *Count-Down*, New York: Karz–Coll.

Katsenelinboigen, A. (1977), 'Coloured markets in the Soviet Union', *Soviet Studies*, January.

Kemeny, J. (1982), 'The unregistered economy in Hungary', *Soviet Studies*, July.

Kende, P. (1982), 'The post–1956 Hungarian normalisation', in 'Normalisation Process in Soviet Dominated Central Europe, Hungary, Czechoslovakia and Poland', *See* Brus, Kende and Mlynar 1982.

Kenedi, J. (1981), *Do It Yourself. Hungary's Hidden Economy*, London: Pluto Press.

Kerr, C. (1983), *The Future of Industrial Societies. Convergence or Continuing Diversity*, London: Harvard University Press.

Kerr, C. *et al.* (1973), *Industrialism and Industrial Man*, Harmondsworth: Penguin.

Kersten, K. (1982), *Historia Polityczna Polski 1944–1956*, Warsaw: Wydawnictwo Krąg.

Kisiel, H. (1975), 'Drogi umacniania równowagi rynkowej', *Nowe Drogi*, December.

Konrad, G. and I. Szelenyi (1979), *The Intellectuals on the Road to Class Power*, Brighton: Harvester Press.

KOR (1978a), 'Notes on Poland economic situation: an inside view', Trans. and pub. by *RFE Research*, Background report /177 (Poland), 9 August.

KOR (1978b), 'An Appeal to Society, of October 10th 1978', *RFE Research*, PAD Background Report 236, (Poland), 31 October.

Korboński,A. (1972), 'Comparing liberalization processes in Eastern Europe', *Comparative Politics*, January.

—— (1974), 'Prospects for change in Eastern Europe', *Slavic Review*, June.

Korda, B. (1976), 'A decade of economic growth in Czechoslovakia (1962–73)', *Soviet Studies*, October.

Kosiński, B. and J. Wołoszyn (1981), 'Racje i nieporozumienia', *Życie Gospodarcze*, 7 July.

'Koszty utrzymania w latach siedemdziesiątych. Publikacje Głównego Urzędu Statystycznego' (1981), *Trybuna Ludu*, 26 March.

Kozłowski, M. (1980), 'Przywileje miejsca pracy', *Życie Literack-*

ie, 13 April.

Kramer, J. M. (1977), Political corruption in the USSR', *Western Political Quarterly*, June.

Krasucki, L. (1981), 'Przyczynek do analizy kryzysu', *Życie Warszawy*, 29 January.

Krawczewski, A. (1981), 'Socjalizm-biurokracj-reforma', *Polityka*, 31 January.

Krejci, J. (1976). 'Classes and élites in socialist Czechoslovakia' in *The Social Structure of Eastern Europe*. See Faber 1976.

Kryński, M. J. (1978), 'Poland 1977: The emergence of uncensored literature', *The Polish Review*, vol. XXIII, no.2.

Krzak, M. (1981), Błędy w systemie i rozumowaniu. *Polityka-Export-Import*, 21 February.

'The Kubiak report', (1982), *Survey*, Summer.

Kunn, V. V. (1980), 'Eastern Europe in the 1970s', *Slavic Studies*, no.25.

Kurczewski, J. (1981), 'W oczach opinii publicznej', *Kultura*, 1 March.

―――― (1982), 'The old system and the revolution', in *Crises and Conflicts*. See *Crises and Conflicts*.

Kuroń, J. (1977), 'Reflections on a program of action', *The Polish Review*, vol. XXII, no.3.

Kuroń, J. and K. Modzelewski (1969), *An Open Letter to the Party*, London: International Socialist Publications.

Kusin, V. V. (1976), 'The overview of East European reformism', *Soviet Studies, July*.

―――― (1978), 'Ten years after the Prague Spring: Lessons for Eastern Europe', in *International Journal*, Canadian Institute of International Affairs, Autumn.

―――― (1980), 'Eastern Europe in 1970s', Slavic Studies, no.25, Sapporo (Japan).

―――― (1982), 'Husak's Czechoslovakia and economic stagnation', *Problems of Communism*, May–June.

Kuszko, A. (1978), 'Uciekający efekt (polityka płac)', *Życie Gospodarcze*, 17 December.

Kux, E. (1980), 'Growing tensions in Eastern Europe', *Problems of Communism*, March–April.

Kwiatkowski, P. and T. Żukowski (1981), 'Meandry równości', *Polityka*, 21 March.

Ładosz, J. (1983), 'Kształty przeszłości', *Tu i Teraz*, 8, 15, 22 December.

Łakomski, Z. (1981), 'Próba diagnozy', *Trybuna Ludu*, 29 July.

Lamentowicz, Z. (1981), 'Dyskusja: narodziny i zgon polskiego października', *Polityka*, 24 October.

Lane, D. (1976), *The Socialist Industrial State: Towards a Political Sociology of State Socialism*, London: Allen & Unwin.

—— (1982), *The End of Social Inequality? Class, Status and Power under State Socialism*, London: George Allen & Unwin.

Latoszek, M. (1981), 'Jak doszło do Sierpnia', *Czas*, 12 July.

Leslie, R. *et al.* (1980), *The History of Poland since 1963*, Cambridge: Cambridge University Press.

'The letter of 59 intellectuals to the Speaker of the Diet of the Polish People's Republic,' (1976), *The Polish Review*, vol. XXI, nos. 1–2.

Lewyckyj, B. (1981), 'Mechanizmy integracji krajów socjalistycznych', Paris: *Kultura*, January–February.

'Liczy się każdy hektar' (1980), *Słowo Powszechne*, 17 December.

Lipski, J. J. (1983), *Komitet Obrony Robotników KOR*, London: Aneks Publishers.

Malanowski, J. (1981), 'Rozmowa o Nierówności', *Kulisy*, 19 July.

Manteuffel, R. (1981), 'Siła w rozmaitości', *Polityka*, 21 February.

Markiewicz, W. (1981), 'Próba marksistowskiej analizy kryzysu', *Życie Warszawy*, 21 and 22 March.

Markus, G. (1981), 'Planning the crisis: remarks on the economic system of Soviet-type societies', *Praxis*, October.

Matejko, A. (1974), *Social Change and Stratification in Eastern Europe*, New York: Praeger Publishers.

—— (1980), 'Kryzysy strukturalne i ich konsekwencje', *Tygodnik Powszechny*, 20 July.

Matthews, M. (1978), *Privilege in the Soviet Union*, London: Allen & Unwin.

Mieczkowski, B. (1975), *Personal and Social Consumption in Eastern Europe*, New York: Praeger Publishers.

—— (1978), 'The relationship between changes in consumption and politics in Poland', *Soviet Studies*, April.

—— (1979), 'The political economy of consumption in Poland', *The Polish Review*, vol. XXIV, no.3.

Mieszczankowski, M. (1980), Kryzys w gospodarce—przyozny i drogi wyjścià. *Nowe Drogi*, December.

—— (1982), 'Struktura społeczna', *Życie Gospodarcze*, 18 July.

—— (1984), 'Dekompozycja systemu (1971-1990)' *Życie Gospodarcze*, 15 July.

Mikołajczyk, Z. (1980), 'Nad problemami gospodarki lat 50tych', *Życie Gospodarcze*, 5 October.

—— (1981), 'O kryzysie uwagi elementarne', *Życie Gospodarcze*, 12 July.

Miszułowicz, B. (1981), 'Enigmy kryzysu mięsnego ciąg dalszy', *Życie i Nowoczesność*, 15 January.

Mitchell, T. R. (1982), *People in Organizations*, New York: McGraw-Hill International.

Mlynar, Z. (1983), *Relative Stabilization of the Soviet Systems in the 1970s*, Study no.2. Research project: Crises in Soviet-type systems.

Montias, J. (1974), 'Types of Communist economic systems' in *Change in Communist System*. *See* Johnson 1974.

Morawski, W. (1981), 'The peculiarities of the Polish revolution: the system of articulation of interests as a condition of social equilibrium' in *Crises and Conflicts*. *See Crises and Conflicts*.

———— (1983a), 'Wstęp, czyli parą uwag o wzajemnych zwięzkach demokracji i gospodarki' in *Demokracja i Gospodarka*. *See* Morawski 1983b.

———— (ed.) (1983b), *Demokracja i gospodarka*, Warsaw, Uniwersytet Warszawski, Instytut Socjologii.

Morecka, Z. (1981), 'Rozpiętość poziomów spożycia a kwestia socjalistycznej sprawiedliwości społecznej', *Nowe Drogi*, nos.1–2, January–February.

Morrison, J. (1968), *The Polish People's Republic*, Baltimore: Johns Hopkins University Press.

Mozołowski, A. (1980a), 'Dopłacać: Kto? Komu? Za co?, *Polityka*, 3 May.

———— (1980b), 'Pod naciskiem', Polityka, 22 November.

Narojek, W. (1982), 'Struktura społeczna w doświadczeniu jednostki', Warsaw: Państwowy Instytut Wydawniczy.

Nelson, D. (1978), 'Political convergence: an empirical assessment', *World Politics*, vol. XXX.

———— (1981), 'Worker–Party conflict in Romania', Problems of Communism, September–October.

Nelson, D. (ed.) (1983), *Communism and the Politics of Inequalities*, Lexington, Mass.: Lexington Books.

'Nierówności i niesprawiedliwości społeczne w swiadomorści społeczeństwa polskiego', OBOP i SP, *Polish Press Summary*, RFE, 147, 31 July 1981.

Nove, A. (1975), 'Is there a ruling class in the USSR?', *Soviet Studies*, October.

Nowak, J. (1982), 'Church in Poland', *Problems of Communism*, January and February.

Nowak, S. (1976), 'Like Father, Like Son?' *Polish Perspectives*, vol. XIX, July–August.

———— (1980a), 'Value system of the Polish society', *The Polish Sociological Bulletin*, no.2 (50).

———— (1980b), 'A decent person and higher necessity', *Survey*, Winter.

——— (1981), 'Dylemat więźnia', *Kultura*, 27 September.

Nuti, D. M. (1981), 'Poland: economic collapse and socialist renewal', *New Left Review*, November–December.

'Obraz tygodnia', (1981), *Tygodnik Powszechny*, 12 July.

O'Hearn, D. (1980), The consumer second economy: size and effects', *Soviet Studies*, April.

Osnos, P. (1977), 'The Polish road to Communism', *Foreign Affairs*, October.

Ozonek, S. (1981), 'Zanim zasiądziemy do stołu', *Polityka*, 21 March.

Pajestka, J. (1981), *Polish Crisis 1980–81*, Warsaw: Książka i Wiedza.

Pańkow, W. (1982), 'The roots of the Polish Summer: a crisis of the system of power' in *Crises and Conflicts*. See *Crises and Conflicts*.

——— (1983), 'Gospodarka i system społeczno-polityczny PRL: trzy modele rozwiązań' in *Demokracja i Gospodarka*. See Morawski 1983b.

Papiernik, B. (1979), 'Mechanizmy awansu', *Głos Pracy*, 2 October.

Parish, W. (1981), 'Egalitarianism in Chinese Society', *Problems of Communism*, January–February.

Paul D. W. and M. D. Simon, (1981), 'Poland today and Czechoslovakia 1968' in *Problems of Communism*, September–October.

Pazio, M. (1979), 'Konsumpcja społecana i indywidualna. Relacje wzajemne', Warsaw: 1979, Instytut Handlu Wewnętrznego, review in: *Życie Gospodarcze*, 25 May.

Pełczyński, Z. A. (1982), *Poland: The Road From Communism*, Oxford: Pembroke College.

Piekalkiewicz, J. (1975), *Communist Local Government*, Athens, Ohio: Ohio University Press.

Piekarska, I. (1980), 'Zdrowie na złotówki przeliczone', *Tygodnik Demokratyczny*, 5 October.

Podemski, S. (1979), 'Co dziesiąty w administracji', *Polityka*, 26 May.

Pohorille, M. (1978), 'Konsumpcja realna', *Życie Gospodaroncze*, 16 April.

Pohorille, M. (1979), 'Problemy rozwoju konsumpcji indywidualnej i zbiorowej', *Nowe Drogi*, February.

Poland. The State of the Republic, (1981), The reports by the Experience and Future Discussion Group (DiP), London: Pluto Press.

Polish Press Agency (PAP) (1981), text of report (in English) on investigative proceedings, 17 March, *Summary of World Broadcasts*, EE/6677/B/14.

Portes, R. (1977), 'East Europe's debt to the West: interdependence is a two-way street', *Foreign Affairs*, July.

——— (1978), Inflation under central planning' in F. Hirsch and J. H. Goldthorpe (eds), *The Political Economy of Inflation*, Oxford: Martin Robertson.

——— (1980), 'Effects of the world economy crisis on the East European economics', *The World Economy*, vol. 3, no.1, June.

Prawda, A. (1979), 'Industrial workers: patterns of dissent, opposition and accommodation' in *Opposition in Eastern Europe*, See Tőkes 1979.

——— (1982), 'Poland 1980: from "Premature Consumerism" to labour solidarity', *Soviet Studies*, April.

Radgowski, M. (1977), 'Nastroje społeczne', *Polityka*, 24 December.

Raina, P. (1978), *Political Opposition in Poland: 1954–1977*, London: Poets and Painters Press.

——— (1981), *Independent Social Movements in Poland*, London: London School of Economics.

Rakowski, M. (1981a), *Rzeczypospolita na progu lat osiemdziesiątych*, Warsaw: Polish Scientific Publishers.

——— (1981b), *Od Sierpnia do Grudnia, Listy do Mieczysława F. Rakowskiego*, Warsaw: Czytelnik.

Rumer, B. (1982), 'Soviet investment policy: unresolved problems', *Problems of Communism*, September–October.

Rupnik, J. (1979), 'Dissent in Poland, 1968–1978; the end of revisionism and the rebirth of civil society' in *Opposition in Eastern Europe. See* Tőkes 1979.

Rychard, A. (1983), 'Władza i gospodarka—trzy perspektywy teoretyczne', in Morawski (ed.), *Demokracja i Gospodarka.*

Rymuszko, M. (1981), 'W kręgu partyjnej odpowiedzialności', *Prawo i Życie*, 22 March.

Sabbat, A. (1981), 'End of bonanza for Polish party officials?' *RFE Background Report* 58 (Poland), 26 February.

Sakwa, G. (1978), 'The Polish "October": a re-appraisal through historiography', *The Polish Review*, vol. XXIII, no.3.

Sanford, G. (1983), *Polish Communism in Crisis*, London: Croom Helm.

S.C. (1983), 'Biedni ale zdrowi?' *Życie Gospodarcze*, 7 August.

Schapiro, L. (ed.) (1972), *Political Opposition in One-Party States*, London: Macmillan.

Schermerhorn, R. A. (1964), *Society and Power*, New York: Random House.

Schneidermann, S. L. (1959), *The Warsaw Heresy*, New York: Horizon Press.

Schöpflin, G. (1981), 'The political structure in Eastern Europe as a factor in intra-bloc relations' in *Soviet–East European Dilemmas*. *See* Dawisha and Hanson 1981.

────── (1982), 'Poland and Eastern Europe:impact of the Crisis' in *Policy and Politics in Contemporary Poland*. *See* Woodall 1982.

Schwarz, H. (1973), *Eastern Europe in the Soviet Shadow*, London: Abelard Schuman.

Scott, J. (1972), *Comparative Political Corruption*, Englewood Cliffs, N.Y.: Prentice Hall.

Secomski, K. (1971), 'Nowa koncepcja planu 5-letniego, *Nowe Drogi*, no.5.

Shapiro, J. and P. Połichnyj (eds) (1976), *Change and Adaptation in Soviet and East European Politics*, New York: Praeger Publishers.

Shatz, M. (1980), *Soviet Dissident in Historical Perspective*, London: Cambridge University Press.

Shoup, P. (1981), *The East European and Soviet Data Handbook: Political, Social and Developmental Indicators, 1945–1975*, New York: Columbia University Press.

Sik, O. (1980), *The Communist Power System*, New York: Praeger Publishers.

Simes, D. (1975), 'The Soviet Parallel Market', *Survey*, Summer.

Simis, K. (1977–8), 'The machinery of corruption in the Soviet Union', *Survey*, Autumn.

────── (1982), *USSR: the Corrupt Society. The Secret of Soviet Capitalism*, New York: Simon and Schuster.

Simon, D. and R. Kanet (eds) (1981), *Background to Crisis: Policy and Politics in Gierek's Poland*, Westview Special Studies, Colorado: Westview Press.

Simon, J. (1983), *Cohesion and Dissension in Eastern Europe*, New York: Praeger Publishers.

Siwoń, B. (1983), 'Reforma w skali mikro', *Polityka*, 8 January.

Skalski, E. (1979), 'Korzyści i opłaty w naturze', *Polityka*, 22–29 December.

Skilling, Gordon H. (1976), *Czechoslovakia's Interrupted Revolution*, Princeton, N.J.: Princeton University Press.

Słomczyński, K. and T. Krauze (eds) (1978), *Class Structure and Social Mobility in Poland*, New York, White Plains: M. E. Sharpe.

Smolar, A. (1983), 'The rich and the powerful', in A. Brumberg (ed.), *Poland. Genesis of a Revolution*, New York: Vintage Books.

Staar, R. (1982), *Communist Regimes in Eastern Europe*, Stanford, Calif.: Hoover Institution Press.

Staats, S. (1972), 'Corruption in the Soviet System', *Problems of Communism*, January–February.

Staniszkis, J. (1982), 'Self-limiting revolution (one year later)', in *Crises and Conflicts*.

―――― (1983), '"Solidarność" jako związek zawodowy i ruch społeczny', *Demokracja i Gospodarka*. *See* Morawski 1983b.

Strzała, M. (1979), 'Poł życia w akademiku', *Życie Literackie*, 4 March.

Sufin, Z. (1980), 'Społeczne uwarunkowania i konsekwencje kryzysu', *Nowe Drogi*, no.12, December.

―――― (1983), 'Ucieczka w kartki', *Życie Gospodarcze*, 31 July.

Summerscale, P. (1982), *The East European Predicament*, London: Gower.

Świderski, M. (1981), 'Czy jest sposób na PGR y', *Życie i Nowoczesność*, 26 February.

Syrop, K. (1957), *Spring in October*, London: Weidenfeld and Nicolson.

Szczepański, J. (1970), *Polish Society*, New York: Random House.

Szefler, S. (1983), 'Reforma a struktura gospodarcza', *Rzeczywistość*, 10 July.

Szeliga, Z. (1975), 'Mięso—kłopoty i perspektywy'. *Polityka*, 15 March.

Tampke, J. (1983), *The People's Republic of Eastern Europe*, London: Croom Helm.

Taylor, F. and O. Lange (1938), *The Economic Theory of Socialism*, Minneapolis: University of Minnesota Press.

Tőkes, R. L. (ed.) (1979), *Opposition in Eastern Europe*, London: Macmillan.

Triska, J. and Ch. Gati (eds) (1981), *Blue Collar Workers in Eastern Europe*, London: Allen & Unwin.

Triska, J. and P. Cocks (eds) (1977), *Political Development in Eastern Europe*, New York: Praeger Publishers.

Turcan, J. (1977), 'Observations on retail distribution in Poland', *Soviet Studies*, January.

Tymowski, A. (1979a), 'Kto ma pieniądze', *Czas*, 16 December.

―――― (1979b), 'Reguły krajania chleba', *Polityka*, no.46.

UN Statistical Yearbook (1977), Geneva: International Labour Office.

Vajda, M. (1981), *The State and Socialism. Political Essays*. London: Alison and Busby.

Volgyes, J. (ed.) (1975), *Political Socialization in Eastern Europe:*

A Comparative Framework, New York: Praeger Publishers.

Wacowska, E. (1971a), *Poznań 1956—Grudzień 1970*, Paris: Institut Littéraire.

――― (1971b), *Rewolta Szczecińska i jej znaczenie*, Paris: Institut Littéraire.

Waterbury, J. (1973), 'Endemic and planned corruption in a monarchical regime', *World Politics*, vol. 25, no.4.

Weinberg, I. (1969), 'The problem of convergence in industrial societies', *Comparative Studies in Society and History*, vol. 11, no.1

Wellisz, S. (1964), *The Economies of the Soviet Bloc*, New York, London: McGraw-Hill.

Welsh, W. A. (1976), 'Élites and leadership in Communist systems: some new perspectives', *Studies in Comparative Communism*, vol.IX.

Werblan, A. (1968), 'Przyczynek do genezy konfliktu', *Miesięcznik Literacki*, June.

――― (1981), 'Dawne kryzysy i dzisiejsze problemy', *Życie Warszawy*, 13 January.

Weschler, L. (1982), *The Passion of Poland*, New York: Pantheon Books.

Wesołowski, W. (ed.) (1970), *Struktura i Dynamika Społeczeństwa Polskiego*, Warsaw: Polish Scientific Publishers.

――― (1972), 'The notions of strata and class in socialist society' in A. Beteille (ed.), *Social Inequality*, Harmondsworth: Penguin Books.

――― (1980) in J, Danecki (ed.), *Towards Poland 2000. Problems of Social Development*, Warsaw: Zakład im Ossolińskich.

―――Wesołoski, W. and K. M. Słomczyński (1977), *Investigations on Class Structure and Social Stratification in Poland, 1946–1975*, Warsaw: Institute of Philosophy and Sociology (PAN).

Westoby, A. (1981), *Communism since World War II*, Brighton: Harvester.

Weydenthal, J. B. de (1977), 'Party development in contemporary Poland', *East European Quarterly*, vol.XI.

――― (1978), *The Communists of Poland: An Historical Outline*, Stanford, Calif.: Hoover Institution Press.

――― (1979a), *Poland: Communism Adrift*, Beverley Hills/London: Sage Publications.

――― (1979b), 'The workers' dilemma of Polish politics: a case study', *East European Quarterly*, vol. XIII, no.1.

Widera, W. (1983), 'Stare związki zawodowe wobec potrzeb

pracowniczych' in *Demokracja i Gospodarka*. *See* Morawski 1983b.

Więcei y prawdy o inwestycjach, Z materiałów GUS'u', *Życie Gospodarcze*, 5 July 1981.

Wilczyński, J. (1972), *Socialist Economic Development and Reform*, London: Macmillan.

Winiecki, J. (1982), 'Cykle inwestycyjne a inflacja popytowa w gospodarce planowej', *Ekonomista*, 5–6.

Wołosiuk, L. (1981), 'Ziemia musi rodzić', *Kultura*, 11 January.

Woodall, J. (1982), *The Socialist Corporation and Technocratic Power*, London: Cambridge University Press.

Woodall, J. (ed.) (1982), *Policy and Politics in Contemporary Poland. Reform, Failure and Crisis*, London: Frances Pinter.

Woś, A. and J. Zegar (1980), 'Problemy finansowania rozwoju rolnictwa', *Nowe Drogi*, no.5, May.

Wrong, D. H. (1979), *Power. Its Forms, Bases and Uses*, Oxford: Basil Blackwell.

Wrzaszczyk, T. (1980), 'Dyskusja' in *Nowe Drogi*, nos.10–11, October–November.

Zabrzewski, R. (1975), 'Wzrost dochodów i zmiany struktury spożycia', *Nowe Drogi*, September.

Żarski, T. (1980), 'Ocena zmian sytuacji mieszkaniowej w latach 1970–78', *Praca i Zabezpieczenie Społeczne*, November.

——— (1981), 'Jak dzielić', *Polityka*, 25 August.

Zasłavsky, Victor (1982), *The Neo-Stalinist State. Class, Ethnicity and Consensus in Soviet Society*, Brighton: Harvester Press.

Zdamiewiez, W. (1979) 'Kościół Katolicki w Polscie 1945–79', Poznań-Warsaw: Palladinum.

Zinner, P. (ed.) (1956), *National Communism and Popular Revolt in Eastern Europe*, New York: Columbia University Press.

Zinoview, A. (1984), *The Reality of Communism*, London: Victor Gollancz.

Zrozmów z Kazimierzem Tyrańskim, Argumenty, 5 April 1981.

Żurek, E. (1981), 'Kariera J. H. Z całą odpowiedzialnością', *Argumenty*, 15 November.

Żurkowie, W. and E. (1918), 'Nie po drodze', *Argumenty*, 26 August.

Index